Kaarlo Syväntö

Kaarlo Syväntö
Pioneer in Israel 1947–1998

Unto Kunnas

Second Edition
Edited by Natalie King

Resource *Publications*

An imprint of *Wipf and Stock Publishers*
199 West 8th Avenue • Eugene OR 97401

KAARLO SYVÄNTÖ

Copyright © 2006 Olavi Syväntö. Published in cooperation with the John Haller Institute. All rights reserved. Except for brief quotations in critical publications or reviews, no part of this publication may be reproduced in any manor without prior written permission from the John Haller Institute. Write: Permission, John Haller Institute, 210 Constitution Ave., Goshen, IN, 46526. Or email: Permission (in subject header), info@johnhallerinstitute.org.

Wipf & Stock Publishers
199 W. 8th Ave., Suite 3
Eugene, OR 97401

ISBN: 1-59244-563-2

Manufactured in the U.S.A.

Contents

Author's Preface ix
Editor's Comments xii

Chapter 1: The Preparatory Years 1
    My First Job ~ A Shocking Discovery ~ Bribes ~ More Fraud ~ Honesty Brings Blessing

Chapter 2: The Lord My Faithful Helper 12
    Psalms 50 Proves True ~ Secret Documents ~ A Close Call ~ Brothers in Reconciliation ~ An Angel of the Lord?

Chapter 3: The Reward of Obedience 19
    Travel Tickets ~ Stolen Luggage ~ Almost a Suicide ~ A Near Crash

Chapter 4: My Promise to the Lord 28
    A Prayer ~ A Glimpse into the Future ~ A Message to the People of Israel

Chapter 5: Signs from Heaven 34
   A Confirmation of the Calling ~ A Land Deal ~ A
   Step Forward ~ A Remarkable Dream ~ The Little
   Ship Sails

Chapter 6: Encouragement in Trials 44
   A Brother with a Similar Calling ~ God Sees my
   Need ~ An Open Door to England

Chapter 7: England 50
   Peeling Potatoes ~ A Pleasant Surprise ~ "To Obey is
   Better than Sacrifice" ~ Sewing Supplies

Chapter 8: Destination Palestine 56
   The Lord my Provider ~ Hurdles to Overcome ~
   My First Special Permit ~ A House in the Galilee
   ~ November 1947 ~ In the Midst of the Battle ~ In
   Mortal Danger ~ Saved Again

Chapter 9: Back to Scandinavia 69
   100-pound Stamps ~ "Smooth Sailing" with the Lord
   ~ The Family Adrift ~ At the Teemassaari School ~
   The Summer of 1948 in Norway ~ Preparing for the
   Return Trip ~ At the Very Last Moment

Chapter 10: Back in the Promised Land 80
   My New Friend the Rabbi ~ Pioneering in Tel Aviv
   ~ Picking Oranges ~ Carrots, Carrots and more
   Carrots! ~ A Different Kind of Job Proposition

Chapter 11: In Tiberias 89
   The Scottish Mission ~ Looking for a Home ~ A
   House on the Lakeshore ~ The Family Arrives ~
   Work Without Pay ~ A Shame and a Disgrace ~
   Sailors in Distress ~ Our Children at Risk ~ Poverty
   ~ A Wolf in Sheep's Clothing

Chapter 12: The Bible Work Begins   105
Shipments of Three Hundred Copies ~ Opposition at Customs ~ My Friend the Rabbi "Saves the Day" ~ A Large-Scale Printing Job ~ In Prestigious Company

Chapter 13: A New Phase in the Work   114
Bibles in the Post ~ The "Bible-Mobile" ~ The Archbishop's Mistake ~ A Trouble-Making Director of Postal Services ~ The Battle for Bibles Continues ~ Another Road-Block

Chapter 14: New Printing Arrangements   125
The Evangeliipress. ~ God's Word for the Arabs

Chapter 15: God's Wisdom and Timing   132
Over-Sized Crates ~ A Strike at the Harbor ~ Excavations ~ Traveling Mercies in North America ~ A Quick Meeting

Chapter 16: Gleanings   139
The Children's Home Director ~ A Fresh Start ~ The Rabbi's Son ~ The Bookshop Owner ~ A Psychiatrist ~ Another "Fig"

Chapter 17: Answers to Prayer   151
God Provides ~ A Bad Accident ~ A Rolling Boulder

Chapter 18: God's Logic   155
Against All Odds ~ Our Homes in Tiberias ~ A Ring in the Sea ~ Contrary to my Plans ~ A Busy Day ~ A Funeral and a Wedding ~ The Work Continues Regardless

Chapter 19: Israel and her Neighbors — 163
    Aggressor or Victim? ~ The Golan Heights ~ Samaria et al. ~ An Abundance of Natural Resources

Chapter 20: God's Plan for Israel — 168
    A Spiritual Re-Birth ~ Eretz Israel. ~ Some Divine Promises ~ The Hula Valley ~ The Lion Statue ~ The Arab Christians ~ An Influx of Immigrants ~ Help for the Poor ~ Sowing the Seed ~ A Prophetic Dream

Epilogue — 180

Author's Preface

I stood on a balcony of the sixth floor of Hotel Galil in Netanya listening to the rhythmic sound of the waves rolling in. It was a dark evening. The street next to the hotel was empty and dimly lighted. On the other side, the sea, where the whitecaps were visible in spite of the darkness.

The evening was warm even though it was the season between late February and early March, and I looked up at the arching heavens, star-studded as far as the eye could see. The same view of the heavens was seen by Abraham, the father of our faith, to whom God had made great promises. Thus I meditated alone, enjoying beyond measure my new surroundings and the stillness which seemed to be deepened by the rhythmic sound of the surf breaking along the shore.

With several tourists, we had rented a taxi for the day. We drove past many places mentioned in the Bible including through the city of Nazareth to Tiberias. From a telephone near the post office I called Syväntö, whom I had known for over thirty years. His wife Maire answered the phone and when I asked her if our entire group could come to visit them for awhile, she replied, "Yes, of course, whenever you like! Kaarlo, too, will be home shortly."

We didn't have much time so we decided to see first the familiar places on the shores of the Sea of Galilee. With our Jewish chauffeur, an excellent guide, we drove past Beit Saida to the ruins of Capernaum. He related the happenings on this beautiful shore during Jesus' time. However, he himself was not a Christian.

Our meeting with the Syväntös had to be a brief one. There were many things to discuss, but somehow the head of the household managed to find time to explain to his guests something about his calling to Israel and his work there.

That evening as I recalled the events of the day, a surprising idea suddenly popped into my mind: Why didn't you even say a single word to Kaarlo that a book should be written about his work? Kaarlo would of course write it himself, but you could do it. Offer to do it!

Twenty years earlier I had written a book about Kaarlo's difficult childhood, published in Finnish under the title, Orpo-Olavin Koettelemukset (Orphan Olavi's Trials). It had had eight printings, all of which had long since been sold out. What would be more natural than for you to ask to continue his story from where it left off earlier? But would he agree? You could ask him.

Regretting my lack of thought, I went to find a telephone. Maire answered, "Kaarlo is at a speaking engagement." I explained my thought to her about writing a book about Kaarlo's work but Maire interrupted saying, "No, no no! He doesn't want man to be praised."

"That is not the purpose," I replied. "A book can be written so that the person remains on the sidelines in order that the Lord be glorified in His great faithfulness to His servant."

"So many," she then said, "have come here to ask Kaarlo's permission to write his biography but he has never agreed."

"Well," I continued, "do tell Kaarlo anyway of my proposal. The very thought of it makes my head spin. John the Baptist was the forerunner for Jesus when He first came into the world. Now we live in a time when our Lord's Second Coming is being realized. Let Kaarlo say what he will, but on the basis of what I know of Kaarlo's work, I think that he has been, and still is, clearing the way in Israel for the Second Coming of our Saviour. It's for that very reason that he has worked these years distributing Bibles by the hundreds of thousands among Israel's own people."

Maire was silent so I continued. "Please speak with Kaarlo about this suggestion. Perhaps he could call me in the morning."

"I'll tell him."

Preface

In the morning, Kaarlo called and in his typical way went straight to the point: "Maire told me you called and I want to let you know that I agree with your proposal. Many have asked my permission for this, but I haven't wanted to give it. You may have it. He who has begun the work (referring to the first book about his life) may continue. Send me cassette tapes. I will record on them. Then let me read the transcript."

–Unto Kunnas

Editor's Comments

It is with great joy that I introduce to you this new edition of Kaarlo Syväntö's biography, in the making since 1997! Many thanks to Chryssie McBrayer who helped "set the wheels in motion" and especially to Kaarlo -or vaari (grandpa) as he was called affectionately by those close to him- for all of his encouragement!

My prayer is that this very personal account of a man's "walk with God" may bring you hope and faith in the God of Israel who cares so much not only for all of the nations of the world but also for each and every individual in His Creation.

It has been a blessing to produce this edition. Not only did God provide the time and inspiration necessary to its completion, He answered my prayer for a laptop computer in the exact manner in which Kaarlo received a typewriter during his stay in England! I received a phone call some weeks after my prayer from a couple who felt that it was time to donate their extra computer to the person God would place in their heart! With God all things are possible.

I would like to clarify the following vocabulary used in the book:

- "Messianic believer" is a widely accepted term for a Jew who believes in Jesus (Yeshua) as the Jewish Messiah of Israel and the whole world, or for a Gentile who identifies him/herself with this manner of expression of faith in God. The term Christian is necessarily avoided due to the

Introduction

misconceptions associated with the word due in large part to its use by anti-Semitic groups throughout history.

- The King James Version of the Bible is used in all quotes, in keeping with the personal preference of Kaarlo Syväntö.

- This book is not intended in any way to propagate negative actions against any person or group of people but rather to encourage mutual respect for each other's background, faith and personal opinion.

Finally, I wish you happy reading! May the Word which became flesh breathe life into the message of this book and bring you a renewed conviction of the one and only Reality Who is closer to us than we often dare to imagine! As it says in Acts 17:24-28:

> God that made the world and all things therein, seeing that he is Lord of heaven and earth, dwelleth not in temples made with hands; Neither is worshipped with men's hands, as though he needed any thing, seeing he giveth to all life, and breath, and all things; And hath made of one blood all nations of men for to dwell on all the face of the earth, and hath determined the times before appointed, and the bounds of their habitation; That they should seek the Lord, if haply they might feel after him, and find him, though he be not far from every one of us: for in him we live, and move, and have our being.

–Natalie King

Chapter 1

The Preparatory Years

My First Job

I was born at Kelva, in northern Karelia. My mother, barely twenty years of age, died of tuberculosis when I was only eight months old. At the time, my father was building the railroad from Joensuu to Nurmes and so he placed me in a Christian home. I thought that I was their child but when my father's contract ended, he came with a new wife to fetch me. My new stepmother turned out to be cruel and heartless, particularly towards her stepchild. For me, childhood was like a bad dream.

At eighteen, I was a successful, tall and skinny seventh grader with the intention of graduating from high school the following year. This idea did not suit my stepmother at all. She would make a fuss and say, in the presence of other people, "He is already such a big, mischievous boy. He should get a job and make a living for himself."

I realized that I had to bury my hopes of a university education, to leave home and my stepmother behind me forever.

But the clothes I owned were not exactly suitable for work interviews. So I went to see a shopkeeper I knew and explained to him my situation. Would he trust me enough to provide a decent suit and shoes? I would pay him as soon as I got a job. The shopkeeper called his wife, and together they clothed me. They were well aware of my difficult childhood.

Then I went to see the Salminen stationmaster and told him of my desire to work in the railroad business. He was willing to help in any way possible, knowing the hardships that I had endured at home. He gave me a letter of recommendation and in November 1927, I was approved as an apprentice. I signed a contract in the city of Mikkeli at the office of the railroad traffic supervisor. I began my training at the Salminen station in January 1928.

In those days, telegrams were sent in Morse code. The telegram dispatcher examination was the first test, consisting of questions on rules and regulations. I passed, and so I got started in my career as a train dispatcher. Soon I was transferred from Salminen to Haapakoski and from there to Iisvesi.

The following autumn, courses in the business of railroading began in Helsinki. Housing was hard to find and rent was expensive, so I had to find a roommate. He turned out to be one who did not exactly take his studies seriously. He drank and in every way lived a worldly life. It took some time before he understood that I wasn't the same type of person. I wanted to prepare myself for my life's work as best as possible, without wasting time in the process.

In the spring of 1929, eighty-seven of us graduated, fully equipped to be competent railroad employees. We received our diplomas according to our grade-rank in the class. Matti Voltti, who was later to become the director of this same course, received four point five out of five -the highest score. I was among the top ten with an average of four.

I was sworn into office and received my first official assignment within the Seventh Traffic Division. Recalling these years of study, I can see the clear guidance of God, even though at the time I didn't yet have a personal relationship with Him.

At the end of the summer of 1929, the heavy Depression years began. Many well-to-do families were forced to sell their homes and large businesses went bankrupt. Even my uncle's farm in Lapinlahti was sold at the auctioneer's gavel.

I must confess that I was disappointed at not having been able to graduate from high school. I had by that time found faith in God and I had asked Him more than once why He had not allowed me to finish my studies – "It's not like the graduate-cap wouldn't have fit my head just like it did the others'," I would tell Him.

Later I understood the Lord's guidance even in this period of my life. Even if I had studied one more year and had become a university student, it wouldn't have helped me at all during the Great Depression. The railroad-training course in which I participated was the last one offered for eight years. And in spite of employee cutbacks, I was fortunate enough always to have a regular position.

I believe that the reason why God thus directed me even before I believed in Him was because of my biological mother's devout prayers.

A Shocking Discovery

"Well now, aren't you the lucky one!" my colleagues remarked when they heard to which station I had been assigned. "The officials there get a lot of extra income which certainly comes in handy! You know the old saying, 'the government's loaf of bread is narrow, but it is long' (although the pay is insignificant the job is secure)." I wondered to myself what the extra income might be.

On the very first day, the manager of a large lumber company greeted me, "Welcome to our neighborhood, Mr. Syväntö! Our factory club has an interesting social evening on Sundays. The station employees are usually there with us. We hope that you too will come and enjoy yourself there."

"We have always had good relations with the folks at the station," he continued. "We take care of your electric bills, we don't even bother to read your meter. And since we have plenty of timber, just tell us where your woodshed is and chopped firewood will be brought to you. And if there is anything else you need, the factory has the resources to help you."

I suspected that something abnormal was going on. At the factory club, the men drank a lot and really "lived it up." I realized that I had to 'lay my cards on the table' immediately and tell the manager about my different way of life. Because if we want to live as Christians we must openly confess our faith, otherwise our lives will be useless.

Kaarlo Syväntö

***

So then faith cometh by hearing, and hearing by the word of God. For with the heart man believeth unto righteousness; and with the mouth confession is made unto salvation (Romans 10:17, 10).

***

So I said to him: "I am a practicing Christian. If I have a free Sunday, I want to hear the preaching of the Gospel or I go to spread the Good News myself. I don't make time on Sundays for anything else."

The manager looked at me in amazement. He must have thought, *What kind of fanatic do we have here, who has come to this station? We can hardly expect to have him as the fourth player in our card games!*

My mind was occupied with wondering what the station employees' additional income could be. Then I was told that during the Christmas season the lumber company gave substantial monetary gifts to all employees at the station, from the stationmaster down to the menial workers. The entire staff of the station was bribed. Everyone's electric bills were paid, firewood was free and the drinks were 'on the house' at the factory club every Sunday evening.

I was a Christian, now being offered the same favors. *What was really behind all this?* I decided to investigate.

First, I went to see the loading of the wood products. I took note that extremely heavy, dripping wet logs were lifted onto the railroad cars. When the loading inspector saw me approaching with a concerned look on my face, he came over to chat with me.

"At this station," he said, "it has been the custom for a long time that the factory prepares the bill of lading so that the station employees don't have to trouble themselves by standing around here for nothing. Of course, we pay the amount specified on the bill of lading."

I began to follow carefully the hustle and bustle of the factory's loading activities. In transporting lumber, several classes of freight are used in its transport. The cost depends on the width of the planks; whether they are un-planed or flawless; and whether their width is more than or less than eleven centimeters. The prime planks for export are in a different class from the un-planed ones.

When I compared the bills of lading with the shipments, the bills of lading did not show the correct figures at all. According to my calculations, the lumber company used some thirty thousand marks for bribes yearly and the state lost about three million marks because the bills of lading were not examined. The bribes were a "good business investment" that gave the lumber company an enormous profit.

Satan tried intimidating me with the thought: *Are you aware of the consequences if you act like an undercover policeman exposing the dishonest deeds of so many men? What will this cost you? Even if you won't take bribes yourself, surely you know how to close your eyes when you don't want to see something. Just stick to your own business and dispatch the trains on time.*

But I had a different definition of moral responsibility, and so an hour before the next bill of lading was to be ready, I took a notebook and pencil and went from freight car to freight car, inspecting each one containing lumber. What did I find? The bills of lading were not correct at all. I made my own entries for the separate grades of lumber and their weight. My results were altogether different from those entered on the bill of lading. I also noticed another kind of fraud. At the center of a car there were prime, planed planks for export and on top of these were placed rough, un-planed planks which provided at the same time a roof for that car. The entry on the bill of lading indicated that the freight was defective lumber, transported by rail at a lower rate. Having the bills of lading in my possession, I corrected them one by one.

The only difficulty was that I couldn't verify the weight of the cars. The Railroad Commission had recommended a scale for our station, with which everything could be accurately weighed. When the director of the lumber company heard of it, he panicked and invited the stationmaster to the company club where he entertained him, in style. After that, the stationmaster wrote the Commission that they could manage quite well without the scale: *Buying a scale would be an unnecessary expense for the country at a time of financial difficulties. A railroad car scale wasn't really an absolutely necessary piece of equipment.* On the basis of that letter, the scale had not been acquired. The lumber company manager was satisfied.

But I didn't have to automatically approve of the weight indicated on the bill of lading. Once, the manager brought me an enormous stack of bills of lading. I knew that they contained heavy freight because wet logs had been loaded directly onto the cars. They had marked the weights, according to *their* calculations, as much lighter than they actually were. I thought this over for a moment and then wrote on the bill of lading: "To be weighed en route! Weight to be reported to the departure station."

The cars were weighed at Mikkeli before they continued on to Kotka.

"What were the weights of those cars?" I asked when I called the Mikkeli station.

"We're getting incredible loads from your station!" was the reply. "In the small cars, whose capacity is ten tons, there were loads of nineteen and a half and even twenty tons. The regulations permit ten percent above the specified limit but you are running cars with double loads. This must not be!" he warned. "There is an obvious danger that axles will break and bearings will burn out. A railroad accident could occur at any time. You people don't have any sense regarding the loading of freight."

"True enough," I answered. "All overweight cars from here are to be reloaded properly there and the extra costs are to be billed to the company here."

Bribes

That is what we did. When the lumber company received the freight bills, the manager was distraught. He came to the station one day when I was on duty alone and began to chat somewhat distractedly.

"Excuse me, Mr. Syväntö, but you were away at Christmas time, when the others received some Christmas gifts. I'll take care of that matter right now." He placed a fairly thick, brown envelope on my table and walked out of the room.

I examined the contents of the envelope. Out fell bill after bill - totaling an amount that equaled five months of my salary. He must have thought it possible to stuff money into the mouth of a difficult employee in order to keep it shut.

I took a memo-pad and wrote: "I get my salary from the state. I have taken an official oath by which I am committed to conducting business conscientiously and in accordance to the law. Therefore I am returning the enclosed money. In addition I want to say that as a Christian, I will not under any circumstances sell my conscience. I will always strive to fulfill my duties honestly and according to the law, whatever those duties may be."

When I got off duty that evening, I went to the manager's home and rang the doorbell. When his wife opened the door, I handed her the envelope and simply said, "Greetings to the manager."

At the factory they weren't quite sure what to do about me. They seemed to me like dogs with their tails between their legs - but the quiet didn't last long.

One day the lumber company manager came into our office when the stationmaster 'happened' to be at his desk. Apparently they had a plan destined to take care of this young lad. The manager offered the stationmaster and myself a cigar. "Thank you, I don't smoke," I replied.

The gentlemen puffed at their cigars for a while and then spoke. "Listen, Mr. Syväntö! We have always gotten along well with employees at this station but you are an entirely incorrigible case!" In front of me lay a thick pile of bills of lading, bills that I had examined. The atmosphere was tense. I decided to face it head-on. I looked straight into the eyes of the manager who had stepped close to my desk.

"Do you understand that you are the youngest at this station?" he asked. "And you don't even have a permanent appointment here. My firm is the largest commercial user of this station and I can file a complaint that you have not treated us with the courtesy and respect that we deserve." You could be easily transferred elsewhere. Do you understand what this is all about?"

I rose slowly from my chair. My cheeks reddened a bit. When I have to deal with unscrupulous people - and there have been enough of these along the way - I don't give up or negotiate and compromise with them. I 'take the bull by the horns'.

I answered slowly and forcefully, "Listen now, gentlemen! No power in the world can force me to sign my name on falsified documents. Not even my superior can force me to do that. On the contrary, I will complain to the Commission and request an investigation into the affairs of this station to find out who is doing his job properly and who is not. Should we continue, gentlemen? If this station continues in the same manner of operation I will definitely make a complaint and this matter will be investigated in depth. Then it will be clear who has been deceitful and who has not."

The gentlemen were shocked. The stationmaster scampered quickly to his own room and the lumber company executive couldn't remember where he had left his hat. When he finally found it, he walked out without saying another word. I was left alone on the so-called "battlefield" with the bills of lading.

More Fraud

But the saga continued. New plots were concocted on Sunday evening at the factory club. One day, the stationmaster reported that a twenty-percent reduction on transporting sawdust had been granted the lumber company. He mentioned the number of the memorandum that was to be recorded on the bill of lading. He didn't show me the memorandum and I didn't look into it.

Quite a large number of sawdust cars traveled to their destination to the Kotka harbor. I am not sure what length of time elapsed, perhaps half a year, when an inner voice told me, *Look into that sawdust car matter!*

I wrote to the Railroad Commission and asked for a copy of the memorandum. It read as follows:

> The ***firm has been granted a twenty percent reduction in the transport of sawdust cars under the following conditions:
> 1) The sides of the cars are to be made of detachable loose boards of discarded lumber;
> 2) The cars are to stay empty for use at the stations of destination that will avoid the transportation of empty cars and thus a twenty- percent saving to the lumber company.

I checked to see whether or not the orders in the memorandum had been followed. The stationmaster had given permission for about twenty large cars to be used for this purpose but I discovered they were state-owned cars -with the firm's name inscribed on them! As they appeared to be privately owned, they were automatically returned to the station of departure. Others experienced a shortage of cars, but the lumber company did not because they now had twenty state-owned cars illegally labeled with the firm's name!

I called the transport inspector's office in Mikkeli and explained the situation.

"My good fellow!" he exclaimed, "You are responsible, having authorized the bill of lading. Why didn't you take care of it?"

"I've been deceived," I replied. "The memorandum reached me a moment ago. Earlier I knew only the number of the memorandum."

"Well, take care of the matter the way you see fit. We won't interfere in any way."

I wrote to the Commission that the requirements in the memorandum had not been followed. Twenty cars made the round trip even though they should have stayed at their destination. Also, the instructions for the sides of the freight cars had not been carried out.

The letter caused a bomb-like reaction. Two days later, a telegram arrived from the Railroad Commission to every station in the country:

> Due to certain reasons, the Ministry of Transportation and Public Works' attention has been drawn to certain abuses in regard to the movements of railroad cars transporting sawdust. From this day on, all rate reductions for such cars are cancelled at all stations in the nation and all sideboards on the cars must be removed immediately.

When this "cancer" was removed, suddenly the national income rose by 10,000 marks. It was a severe blow for the lumber firm, which now had to pay back all the discounts they had received, amounting to a half million marks. One can imagine how frantic the persons involved became. One of my colleagues who had received a permanent appointment to that station scoffed at me, jeering: "No 'real man' would have pulled such a stunt! Our wages are so low and you sawed off the very branch you're sitting on!"

I snapped back, "Listen so you'll know why. I have never intended to sit on a branch where the devil sits! And besides, with this kind of 'business' you'd better believe that your life won't be blessed!"

I applied for and received a transfer to another station. In the process of moving, I met a conductor who complained, "You were the only man at that station who kept things in order and now you are leaving! Now the remaining ones will surely live 'like cows in the clover field' when you leave."

I discovered yet another kind of fraud. Because some freight was to be carried across the lake, a landing pier was used, for which a small fee was charged. But the officials traded the landing fees for eggs, buttermilk, cream, meat, and cloudberries which the commoners and merchants brought them.

Once when a merchant came to claim his belongings, I started to write a bill for the landing fee. The man peered through the window into the room and shouted, "This is a strange station! Sometimes there is a landing fee, and at other times there isn't! Why is it so?"

I looked him straight in the eye and said, "It's because some will accept bribes and others will not! Do you still want to discuss it?"

Red-faced, the man obediently paid what he was supposed to pay.

Honesty Brings Blessing

Four or five years later, I visited that same community. I met an aged, devout sister and inquired, "What has been going on at the station lately? How is the stationmaster? What about the lumber business? Is it flourishing?"

Her response was: "The stationmaster died soon after you left and the lumber company went bankrupt. The manager lost everything he owned, even his own house. In trying to avoid personal property taxes, he had listed his home as business property."

That gave me a shock. It was clearer to me than ever that wrongdoing never pays. Our Lord tells us in His Word that if we surrender something for His Name's sake, we will receive in return "an hundredfold" (Mark 10:28-30). I lost perhaps 10,000 marks by not taking bribes, due to my conscience being in line with the ways of God. How much is one hundred times 10,000? A million! From this time on, God's remarkable blessings accompanied me in financial matters.

Among the locations I was stationed at was Kintaus, near Jyväskylä, shortly before the onset of WWII. I wanted to buy a small lakeside property and build a cabin so that after a difficult night shift, I could go there to relax, fish and rest. The owner told me he wouldn't sell a lot but that he would sell the whole farm! He convinced me to buy a fifty-two-hectare farm of which two hectares had been cultivated. The farm included eight hundred meters of good, sandy lakeshore, plus farmland and buildings. The cooperative credit bank granted me a loan of 100,000 marks at six-percent interest, to be paid in ten years. What we had in savings covered taxes and other expenses. This happened in the summer of 1939.

In order to immediately cut down the size of the bank loan, I sent a lumberjack to mark some trees in our forest to be cut for firewood. To my great surprise, the harvest of logs was many times greater than I had expected.

During the fall of the year when war was threatening our nation, the price of firewood increased so much that the balance of our mortgage was paid off.

In the town council there was a man who had a hostile attitude toward believing Christians. He knew that I was a Christian and he was annoyed that I had so many logs for sale. Other landowners hadn't bothered to cut so many trees for firewood because the demand wasn't normally very great in times of peace.

This man actually set up an order prohibiting me from cutting trees in my forest. It so happened that as war broke out, all forest-owners were required to provide firewood at a low price, as set by the government. Our forest, however, was exempt, thanks to the order made by the jealous town official! I didn't have to cut a single cubic meter of logs!

After this, the same official got into trouble with the police. During the war, while traveling on a train without the proper identification papers, he was locked up in the prisoners' car. When the train arrived at the Kintaus station, he called to me from the window, "Syväntö! Come and identify me so that I can get out of here!"

Of course I identified my "good friend and benefactor" and he was freed.

From the proceeds of the farm we received many times more than what we had lost previously because I wanted to be a Christian and an honest state employee at Haukivuori.

Chapter 2

The Lord My Faithful Helper

Psalms 50 Proves True

When I was a young Christian, God taught me through many difficult situations to trust in Him and to turn to Him for help. It was a kind of school of obedience; sometimes I acted completely in blind faith and against my own desires. Sometimes I would argue with the Lord, vehemently defend my own views and offer counter-arguments. But in the end I always came to realize my mistake, convinced more than ever that it is best to be guided by Him. My decision to obey <u>always</u> brought me to a place of sincere praise to God. The inner voice, which I believe is of God, taught me, sometimes even "took me by the hand" and as I was obedient, I was able to experience the faithfulness of God!

One evening when I worked at the Kymi station, my shift ended at ten o'clock. The following morning I had to be back at work for six. It was January and freezing cold outside. As I left that night, I locked the safe and the ticket drawer and put the keys in the pocket of my uniform. When I got there the next morning the waiting room was packed with people. My job was to open the ticket window and the cash register and to sell tickets. As I put my hand into my coat pocket, I was dumbfounded to find that the keys were not there -although that is where I had put them the night before -or so I thought!

I returned to my living quarters to search for the key. As I went I prayed to the Lord.

The customers were surely wondering why the ticket booth was closed and why I had disappeared. I imagined people were tapping impatiently at the window. So I returned to the office quickly because I knew it was worthless looking for the keys in my apartment.

In desperation I fell on my knees in a corner of the room and anxiously appealed to His promises, saying: "Lord, You say in Your Word, 'Call upon me in the day of trouble: I will deliver thee, and thou shalt glorify me' (Psalms 50:15). Lord, I am in a time of great trouble! I am the only believer in You at this station. If I have indeed lost the keys, there will be a horrible scandal."

"First of all, calm down!" the Lord told me. "Of course I will help you. Place the chair on which you sat last night, in exactly the same place it was when you left for home. Hang up your uniform coat on the hook just as you did last night."

I can't play games now, I thought. *People are wildly pounding at the window.* Nevertheless, I did as He said. I put the chair in its place and the coat on the hook.

"Now, sit down on the chair and go retrieve the keys from the coat pocket!" the Lord said. I obeyed and retraced my steps of the evening before to the clothes rack.

Then I heard: "Put your hand in the pocket and take out the keys!"

I thrust my hand into the pocket and to my great astonishment, the keys were there! I knew for certain that the pocket had been empty since I had turned them all inside-out in my search.

I hurried back to sell tickets, all the while praising God in my heart Who, according to His promise, had helped me in this day of distress. Afterwards, I thought about the mystery of the lost keys. I found a simple and plausible solution. The coat had turned-up cuffs. The cuff and the pocket opening were exactly side-by-side. It must have been that the cuff was on top and the keys landed there instead of in the pocket. When I put everything in place as it had been the night before and put my hand into the pocket, my hand went into the cuff where the keys were. My inner voice instructed me to do just that so that I would find the keys.

Secret Documents

Over the course of my career I found myself in a variety of peculiar predicaments. One of these was during my service at the Kintaus station, to which I was transferred for health reasons.

My job at the Lappila station had become extremely taxing; most of the time, I had to work the night shift as a dispatcher. As a teenager, I had had a hemorrhage of the lungs and a *pneuma thorax*. My heart wasn't in great shape either. The doctor wrote me a letter recommending lighter work, not including night shifts.

I took the letter with me to the director of the Ministry of Transportation and explained the situation.

"You have a permanent position so it will not be a problem," he said. "Let's arrange it this way. You may ask to be transferred wherever you wish, anywhere in Finland. Once you find a suitable location, send the transfer papers to me."

And so I went on a trek to look for a place and found a vacancy at the Kintaus station. The area was beautiful and there was even a lake nearby. It had great potential for the improvement of one's health. I applied and received the transfer.

Kintaus had an elderly stationmaster on the verge of retirement. He had been on sick leave and so I was appointed as the acting stationmaster. The station had been poorly managed. When I opened the cash register, all sorts of papers fell to the floor in a big heap, like hay from a hayloft. As I picked them up, I noticed a certain document with the word "secret" written on it and on the margin of another, the words "extremely secret." The reason for the secrecy: the accounts for Christmas seals had not been audited for several years, not to mention several other matters that had been neglected.

It was a difficult task to organize the papers. I began by dividing the "secret" and "extremely secret" into separate sealed envelopes. This was fortunate because it wasn't many days later that a high-ranking military officer came to the station and demanded an inspection. Imagine the scandal that could have been!

A Close Call

The unmanaged cash register was not the only problem at Kintaus. The son of a certain Swedish-speaking stationmaster worked there. He was a somewhat "less-gifted" member of a rather disreputable family. He had a secondary school education but he had never passed the psychological tests for the railroad course. He nevertheless held on to the dream of working with the railroad and substituted during the summers for vacationing station employees.

One day, two passenger trains were destined to arrive simultaneously at Kintaus station. I sent the boy to the northern switch, one that was not visible from the station because of a curve in the tracks. Besides, bridges and other obstacles obscured the view of the tracks.

I gave the boy clear instructions to turn the switch on time and to guide one of the trains onto a different track. But when the two trains arrived, they were on the same track and with brakes screeching they stopped about one meter apart, right in front of the station! As I stepped outside, with my official red cap on my head, bare arms with clenched fists reached out toward me from the windows of both locomotives.

I sent another station employee to see what had happened to the switch-changer since my orders had not been followed. When the employee reached him, the poor boy remembered his task and turned the switch! At that point, had the train by chance gone into reverse, it would have broken the switch.

There was an immediate investigation and the boy was questioned on whether or not he understood what he should have done. "Yes," he answered. "I was supposed to switch to the other track." "Well, why didn't you do it?" they asked him. "I started to sweep up the place a little and forgot the entire thing!"

The conductor was asked what the switch-changer did when the train passed him. "He just gawked at me with his mouth open and saluted!"

At that point, he could have waved his arms and given the sign to stop, telling them that everything wasn't in order - but his mind wasn't in order! Fortunately a serious accident did not take place.

The boy was given a fine of two thousand marks and ordered to work at tasks where he would never have anything to do with the safety of the trains. He served later at a warehouse in Jyväskylä, carting boxes. For him a career with the railroad remained only a dream.

Brothers in Reconciliation

During the war, rail travel flourished. Normal schedules could no longer be adhered to and often the traffic backlog was horrendous. Freight trains would be sidetracked to wait their turn while first-class, military, hospital and passenger trains were sent through first.

Once I had to hold up a freight train longer than usual. Its conductor came after a while to ask, "Can't we leave yet?"

"No, because the first-class trains have priority" I replied. I was on the phone regarding an important business matter when the man came to complain again.

"No, you can't leave yet! And now shut up, I have an important call!" I snapped.

It seemed as if he didn't pay any attention to what I said but kept on harassing me for the permission to leave. That's when I "blew my top." I ended the call, threw the receiver on the desk, grabbed the man and threw him out the door. He landed in a sitting position on the waiting room floor.

Fortunately there were no other people in the room. I hardly realized what I had just done when I heard a voice within me saying: "You've done a silly thing. Go and ask his forgiveness right now!"

I quickly reopened the door, went to the man, pulled him to his feet and said, "Forgive me for doing such a silly thing. I am a professing Christian and now as a result of my quick temper, I've brought shame to God for being such a poor example…"

"I'm a believer as well," he replied. "I'm chairman of the Christian Railroad Employees' Association!"

Sitting on a bench, we cleared our differences and in the end, we were the best of friends.

The poor conductor had been on the road for more than twenty-four hours and he was impatient because he was hungry! I called a nearby cafe and asked them to serve the man coffee and cake on my account; a minor compensation for my unacceptable behavior and the solution to his problem!

An Angel of the Lord?

Traffic increased tremendously at the Kintaus station during the war. I wanted a transfer once again and so I applied for Ilmajoki. It was approved effective January 1, 1942. Technically the position included accommodations but the station apartment had already been granted to another station employee. I went to a lot of trouble to get enough time off to search for a house for my family. This was arranged but by evening of the next day I had to be back at work.

All day long I went to every possible part of Ilmajoki looking for a suitable place. It seemed to be a futile mission. Ilmajoki had become home for thousands of evacuees and I was told that there was not even a bed left.

I was hungry and exhausted as I hadn't been able to sleep on the train the night before. It was getting close to four o'clock and my time was almost up. It was then that I said to the Lord, "Are Your promises true? You have said: 'If ye abide in me and my words abide in you, ye shall ask what ye will, and it shall be done unto you'. (John 15:7) Listen Lord, You know that I have a wife and four children whom You have given me. We are supposed to come here in the cold of January. We need a home. Right now I want to see if it is true that You care for your own. I've searched all day for a house and I admit that I'm unable to find one here by myself. But for You, everything is possible. You are able to provide a house from nowhere, although everyone says it's impossible. On top of it all, Lord, I have to hurry because my train leaves in three hours."

I knelt on the side of the road and appealed to the Lord's faithfulness and to His possibilities.

Suddenly a little girl came down the road. "Ask her to be your guide," the Lord said.

I told the girl that I needed a pleasant home, preferably somewhere at the edge of the forest with its own spring and perhaps a small garden.

"Well, yes," said the girl, "I know just the place."

"Take me there quickly," I pleaded.

And sure enough, there was a brick home at the edge of the forest. I asked who owned it and the girl said that it was a merchant named Eino Hakala from Ilmajoki.

When we stepped inside, I had the strange impression that they were waiting for me. Instead of renting the house as I had intended, I was able to buy it! The building was still slightly unfinished and so the owner and I came to an agreement in this regard, and I even had time to choose the wallpaper!

Before the three hours was up I had the preliminary ownership papers to a house in my pocket.

But where did that little girl disappear? I wondered. She was nowhere in sight and the owner of the house didn't know who I was talking about.

To this day I believe that the little girl was an angel sent by God. I never saw her again, even though we lived in Ilmajoki for a long time.

Chapter 3

The Reward of Obedience

Travel Tickets

During the war I was a telegraph operator in Ilmajoki. My duties included managing the train tickets; ordering them as required and keeping the books. One day as I was about to order more tickets, a voice inside me said, "When you order tickets for the stations in the vicinity, ask for ten times more than usual." I obeyed the voice and added an additional zero at the end of each order. A huge supply of tickets arrived. When the old stationmaster saw them he was furious and shouted, "This is outrageous. You've ordered too many tickets! You could have ordered fewer now and additional ones later as the need arises."

"Time will tell why I ordered so many. I've only done my duty," I replied.

Older folks will remember the time when Helsinki was bombed. The railroad also suffered damages. Consequently, all stations in the country received this telegram:

The railroad printing press has been completely destroyed. Write out the tickets by hand. New tickets won't be available for at least another six months.

The Ilmajoki station had enough tickets to last until new ones could be printed.

Stolen Luggage

While living in Ilmajoki, I sought a position as manager of the express package office in Jyväskylä. It was a more prestigious position. In actual fact, I was too young for the job, having served the state only seventeen years, but my wife Maire encouraged me to apply, saying, "Since we have a house at Muurame, in central Finland, it would be possible. The Lord is able to do great things and to give you that position. You are qualified for the job anyhow."

I sent my application and requested a list of the other applicants. Over twenty-five names were on the list. Mine was the last since I was the youngest candidate. Dropping the list in the wastebasket, I said to Maire, "Nothing will come out of this."

One of the biggest surprises in my life came when the Railroad Commission sent me a letter in the spring of 1944, containing an appointment to Jyväskylä. During that time someone named Remes was the transportation inspector for the Ninth District in Jyväskylä. I met him at the station. He welcomed me to my new position and said, "To tell you the truth, I didn't recommend you to the post considering your age but what could I do about it since the Commission appointed you? Anyhow, welcome! I don't have anything against you personally!"

He went on: "But I might as well tell you right now that everything at this express office is in sad shape. Every now and then, goods are stolen. You should try to discover who is responsible for the thefts. The state often gets substantial claims when things disappear. Here's a card on which I've written the name and number of the chief of police. You'll need it if you ever manage to get to the bottom of all this."

I promised to do my best and then without further hesitation I spoke to God about my predicament and asked Him for wisdom. *Doesn't your*

The Reward of Obedience

Word say that we should serve You *"according to the grace that is given to us"* (Romans 12:6) *in our ministry?*

I had barely finished praying when my inner voice spoke: "Take your flashlight and go on a little inspection tour of the attic of the station!"

I went to the warehouse and climbed the stairs leading to the attic. There I discovered a suitcase that had been pried open and its contents confiscated. The only remaining "evidence" was a letter in one of the side pockets, written from a bride-to-be to her fiancé. I was shocked to read:

> In this suitcase you will receive the necessary things that we discussed, including your suit. I'm sending it by express delivery so you will receive it on time for the wedding.

The letter was signed and included the sender's address. The contents never arrived at their destination. It was precisely these types of goods that were regularly reported missing.

I was indignant. I wrote a letter to the sender and requested her to meet me at the express office. When she came, I sincerely apologized for what had happened. I suggested we visit the various storerooms to see if she could identify the person who had received her suitcase. We toured around nonchalantly. Afterwards I asked her, "Did you see the person who dealt with you two months ago?"

"Yes," she answered.

"Who was it?"

"The lady who was sitting at the table."

"Are you sure?"

"Yes," she replied.

She gave me the date and the exact time she had sent the suitcase. After examining the work shifts, I noticed that the woman in question had indeed been on duty receiving goods for express delivery. However, instead of taking this particular shipment's papers to the office, she had taken the suitcase to the attic - and the rest is clear.

I advised her to make an accurate list of what the suitcase contained and to ask the state for reimbursement of the lost articles. "Upon receipt of your list I will pass it on for you and you will be compensated," I assured her.

The claim was indeed recognized as legitimate and the woman received compensation.

But there were also other temptations for a thief in the post office, particularly at this time. It was 1944. The Karelians were evacuating their homes and transporting their possessions, sending their family heirlooms and valuables wrapped in clothing. Quite often, when their shipments arrived in Finland, the clothing was intact but the valuables were not. The express office at Jyväskylä had become especially notorious for such incidents.

Food rations also passed through our office. Cheese, butter and sausages were rationed and only small quantities were allowed per person. On one occasion, several kilos of sausage disappeared. An official report had been made but no follow-up investigation carried out.

I had my own suspicions regarding the sausages. *Maybe the same woman who was interested in suitcase contents was also interested in sausages?* One day when she was off duty I peeked into her desk drawer. At the back, under some paper, I found some sausage wrapper. *The woman had taken and eaten the whole sausage herself!* I put the piece of wrapper in my pocket for evidence and began to consider the next step.

I was aware that the woman's life was a sad story. Her husband, an employee of the Vyborg station, had been killed when the city was bombed. Four young children were left in their mother's care. Their home had likewise been destroyed. Out of mercy she had been granted employment at the Jyväskylä express office, as a single-mother and sole-supporter of her family.

What a lamentable situation, I thought. *What will I do now? If I report this crime it will mean that she will be faced with the loss of her job and time in jail. What would become of those four under-aged children when their mother is taken away?*

I went to God with this problem and prayed fervently, *Oh dear Heavenly Father! What should I do now? Solomon asked you for wisdom in ruling over the people of Israel. I need more wisdom now than Solomon. What shall I do with this person? Grant me wisdom in dealing with this situation! An "operation" is needed but the "patient" must not die in the process!*

I had to take care of this matter. One day when her work shift ended, I called the woman into my office. I locked the door and put the key in my pocket. I looked at her straight in the eye and began by saying,

The Reward of Obedience

"When I came to this office I was given the task of preventing thefts and of restoring order. I have discovered one of the main culprits of our problems. Some time ago, a suitcase was brought here which contained a suit as well as some other items. It never reached its destination. I found the suitcase in the station attic and its owner came here and identified you as the clerk who received her suitcase. She is ready to testify against you in court. Another time, several kilos of sausage disappeared and here is some wrapper from that sausage, which I found in your desk drawer. We have enough evidence to incriminate you."

"But," I continued, "I am also aware of your difficult circumstances. You have lost your husband and your home in Vyborg. You have four under-aged children. As for me, I am a professing Christian and in consultation with my Heavenly Father, I've been thinking of the best thing to do in this case."

I continued: "For the sake of your children's future, I have come to this conclusion. You can make a choice right now as to which road to take. You have five minutes in which to decide. If you kneel here at the edge of the sofa and audibly take a solemn oath before God that the stealing will stop, then, for the sake of your children we will leave this secret between God and us."

"On the other hand, if you don't agree to do this, after five minutes I shall call the chief of police, whose number I have ready. From the police station a car will be sent to get you. It means losing your job and going to prison and I don't know what will happen to your children. You choose what your prefer!"

As I was speaking, the woman became deathly white. She dropped to her knees in front of the sofa and stammered in a tearful voice, "I solemnly swear that I will never again steal anything nor take for myself something belonging to another."

I knelt beside her and took her hand and spoke to God: *Dear Heavenly Father. You have heard this person's promise. You have promised to be a Father to orphans and a support to widows. Lord, we leave this matter in your care. Be merciful and enable this mother to raise her children to be honest and help her to keep her promise.*

I got up and said, "Now, keep your lips sealed! I have no legal authority to settle this case in this way. If this affair is exposed, both of us will get into trouble. It's best now that we do not speak at all about the issue. But remember: you have made a solemn oath to God and you must keep that promise. If you know of others who have done the same thing, tell them that this is the only time that mercy was granted. The next time, the police will be dealing with cases of theft and that definitely means imprisonment for those involved."

We became the best of friends and the stealing stopped. The "operation" was successful, thanks to the Lord's mercy. The "patient" survived. When the Lord later called me to Israel to become the "stationmaster" of the Tiberias "station," I said goodbye to the employees and thanked them for their cooperation. I whispered into her ear so that no one else would hear, "Madam, do you remember the promise that you made?"

"Of course I remember," she nodded.

"I don't want to hear sad news from this place after I have left the country. Will this agreement stand firm without my being here?" She nodded again and smiled. We parted friends.

Almost a Suicide

When I was the manager of the Jyväskylä express office, I would travel to and from our home in Ilmajoki. On one of these voyages, I sat in a small second-class compartment, ready to take a nap. As it happened, a fashionable-looking lady sat opposite from me. I was irritated that I wasn't alone after all. Then the Lord spoke to me, "Speak to her at once about Christ and salvation in Him!"

"Listen, Lord," I answered. "It's not appropriate for someone to approach strangers out of the blue. It's a long trip and I'm quite tired. I wouldn't know how to begin. It's not normal to start talking so unexpectedly about this to someone you don't know! Don't you understand, Lord, that people should behave with some courtesy? Who knows, she might get the wrong impression of my intentions since we two are the only ones in this compartment. Not now, Lord, maybe a little later."

"No," the Lord said. "Right now, start speaking!"

I left the compartment and walked along the corridor very restlessly, thinking how I might begin the conversation and at the same time quarreling with God for giving such a sharp order.

The Reward of Obedience

The lady had a very strange look on her face. Suddenly she gathered her belongings and quickly left the train. I was conscience-stricken. Now my duty was left undone. *And why didn't she stay on the train?*

The train's departure was delayed and right before we left, the conductor came into the car, pushing the lady in front of him. She then took the same seat she had before. At that moment the Lord told me again, "Now, right now, you are to witness to that lady about Christ and salvation! No more delays!"

How to begin? I thought feverishly. I no longer considered protesting or disobeying the heavenly voice.

Someone had recently given me an unusual snapshot that was like a picture puzzle. Looking at it carefully, a profile of Christ could be seen. I took it out of my pocket and said, "Excuse me, ma'am, but I've been given a strange picture. Take a look at it. Do you see anyone in it?"

The lady took the picture, turned it around for a while in her hands and then said "No, I can't see anyone in it."

I went on to explain the story behind it. "This picture came out of very strange circumstances. A certain woman had planned to commit suicide. She was very depressed and in a hopeless state and she couldn't see any other option at that time. She went to the woods where she was going to go through with it. But the Lord met her there and gave her new hope, new faith in life. The act was never committed. Later, this woman went back to the same place where God had given her the courage to conquer life's adversities and trials. She wanted to photograph the spot in the woods where she had been sitting. When the film was developed, it was just like a picture puzzle of Christ's face. Look at it once again!"

I showed her the photograph again. The face of Christ was indeed discernible in the midst of the trees. The lady noticed it as well. She looked at me with a serious expression, obviously agitated.

"Do you have a habit of talking to strangers in this way?" she asked.

"No," I answered. "But immediately, as soon as you came into this compartment, the Lord encouraged me to tell you about salvation in Christ. Wretch that I am, I didn't do it. As you may remember, I left for a while -that was to argue with the Lord about his 'command' to speak with you, a complete stranger!"

Tears welled up in the lady's eyes.

"Can you guess why I left this compartment a while ago?" she asked.

"No," I replied.

"My husband and I have decided to get a divorce. We cannot live together any longer. There are too many things that separate us. Nothing unites us anymore. It is impossible to forgive and to ask forgiveness. The only option I could see was to retire myself from the struggles of life. I bought a one-way ticket so that I could be alone for a while and I bought it for a second-class seat. In my handbag I have enough pills to end my days. I planned to take them right after leaving Haapamäki but I was irritated by your presence in this same compartment, hindering my plan. If I had swallowed them here I wouldn't have been able to die in peace."

She continued: "…I was thinking of what to do. Then I realized that the train hadn't left yet, and besides, maybe the pills wouldn't work fast enough and maybe it would be painful. Then a voice told me: *The train hasn't left yet. Go quickly and leave your belongings down at the entrance of the railway car. Then go outside and put your head on the rail next to the wheel. It won't take more than a half-meter's turn of the wheel to go over your neck and it will be all over.* That is just what I did. I went under the train and waited, my neck on the tracks! The conductor came aboard right at that moment and saw me bending down under the car, thinking that I had dropped something there. He took a hold of me as quickly as best as he could and pulled me out from under there, exclaiming, 'Dear lady! The train is about to leave. You are in great danger. Quickly now, out of there and back inside!'"

Of course the conductor didn't understand that the lady was purposely under the car, attempting to commit suicide. The conductor had unknowingly saved the lady's life.

We had time to talk. In the best way that I knew, I told her that Christ is able to repair our broken lives. He can clear up all our marriage problems if we accept Him as our Help. He gives us a new life. Our sins will be forgiven and our hearts will have a peace that outlasts all of life's storms.

Finally I told her in earnest, "Go home again. Tell your husband how miraculously God saved your life. Ask each other for forgiveness and forgive one another. You have a full life waiting for you and as a new person you will be able to adjust to life's many problems in a new way. You will know to guide others who lack hope to the same Source of hope to Whom I have by God's grace tried to lead you. I will pray for you."

The lady had only a one-way ticket to Seinäjoki, the place destined to be the end of her journey in this world. Now her plans had changed! At the Seinäjoki station I went with her to see her off to Helsinki and to say farewell. The former suicide candidate began a new life.

As for me, I was overwhelmingly grateful to God that I had finally obeyed His command. It would have been most dreadful to witness the consequences of my disobedience! Otherwise I would surely have been haunted by guilt for the rest of my days!

A Near Crash

On that same trip another strange thing happened. As the train approached Vesanka, I was extremely tired. Vesanka is the first station from Jyväskylä toward Haapamäki. I was sleeping in the first passenger car. Suddenly I woke up. It was as if an angel had awakened me and my inner voice said, "Out of the train quickly! Hurry!"

I had learned by then to obey when commanded. I went without delay to the platform. We were at a junction point for two trains. The passenger train was waiting for the freight train but the switch had not been turned as it should have been and thus the freight train was coming at us at full speed.

I was the first to realize the danger and called to God in a loud voice, *Dear Heavenly Father! Help us now so that there won't be a potentially fatal crash!*

The conductor of the passenger train noticed the danger and the train's shrill sound filled the air. At the same time the freight train conductor also saw the impending disaster and slammed on the brakes. With wheels screeching, the freight train stopped barely a meter away from the passenger locomotive.

When I got home, Maire asked me where I had been the evening before at such and such a time.

"I was sleeping on the train at the Vesanka station", I replied.

"Did anything unusual happen to you?"

"Yes," I said, "Death was close to me and many others."

"I felt great distress concerning you at that time and prayed, *Lord, help Kaarlo if he is in mortal danger!*"

Chapter 4

My Promise to the Lord

A Prayer

During the time when I was a young railroad employee at Kymi, I had a hemorrhage of the lungs and I suffered from *pneumatic thorax* for a year and a half. Because of my condition, I was released from the army and transferred to the civil service. The illness was healed and later, during the war years of 1942-1944, I was at the Ilmajoki station. It was an especially critical period for our nation. Our front lines had broken at the Karelian Isthmus and Russia threatened the city of Vyborg. There was an urgent need for manpower and all of the physically unfit were called up for a new examination, including myself. This time I was declared fit for military service and I was to be drafted on 23 October 1943.

I walked home that evening in a very pensive mood. I crossed the road and entered the forest. I found a large spruce tree and sitting in its shade, I laid before the Lord my draft papers and I offered to make a "deal" with Him just as King Hezekiah had done one day.

My prayer went like this: *Hear me, Lord. I want to make a sacred promise to You now. If You will free me from the wars of this world, I will give You my holy promise to serve You on Your front lines for my entire life. You may use* me wherever You want and in whatever way You wish. You yourself have said, The harvest is plentiful but the workers are few. If You have too few workers then I want to offer my life in Your service. I mean this promise to be sincere and true. Now I leave this whole matter in Your hands, Lord. Take care of it as You see best.

I didn't dare tell anyone about this promise, not even my wife. After this we went to a prayer meeting. While we were there, a young sister in Christ received a message from the Holy Spirit that said: "I, the Lord, have heard this promise you made under a spruce tree. I will arrange this matter. A place for you has already been found. Be faithful and obedient and I will help you in everything."

I understood that God had received my offer and so I remained quietly waiting for His answer. But the day was quickly approaching. On Monday morning at six I was to make my way to an unknown fate at the Karelian front.

On Sunday evening we invited some friends to our home for a farewell gathering. At around eight o'clock we were on our knees in prayer. The telephone rang. The call was from Seinäjoki. "We have an urgent telegram for Kaarlo Syväntö. Should I read it over the phone?"

"Please do!" I exclaimed. The telegram read as follows:

Kaarlo Olavi Syväntö's orders to enter military service are hereby cancelled. He will return to service with the railroad.
Signed: The General Committee

This news was certainly worthy of our many thanks to God! We praised Him that He had done such a great miracle.

The explanation: Ilmajoki was an important ammunition station. The old, about-to-retire stationmaster was often ill, leaving me in charge. The railroad had a shortage of employees overall. The Railroad Commission had always taken an interest in my case and had insisted that it was not common sense to send the assistant stationmaster of an ammunition supply station to serve as an inexperienced soldier at the battlefront. They had said, "We cannot give up this man. He is here serving in a much more important position." I was there for the duration of the war.

It was from there that I was appointed to the Jyväskylä station.

A Glimpse into the Future

I was now bound to my promise to the Lord. I went to work in Jyväskylä but my family continued living in our home in Ilmajoki. One evening while I was in prayer before the Lord, an angel suddenly appeared in my room and asked me, "Do you remember the promise you made to the Lord?"

"I remember," I answered.

"The Lord has sent me to show you your future field of work." It was as if he took me by the hand, and we rose through the clouds to some place very far away.

Then he showed me the land to which I had been called. Even from high up I could see that it was definitely empty and barren, without forests, without trees, where no lakes nor rivers could be seen in any direction.

We descended to the surface of the earth. I asked the angel, "What is this land and what is God's purpose in sending me there? What do I have to do there?" I noticed to my great dismay that it was an enormous cemetery full of burial mounds.

The angel answered, "This is an ancient Jewish cemetery. The Lord has given you the task of spreading the joyful Gospel of Christ to those who rest here. That is your task."

I could only exclaim, "But these have already had their time of grace! They are all dead! Something is wrong. This can't be true. God surely doesn't give a second time of grace to anyone."

In the middle of the cemetery there was a large building, like a synagogue. Seeing it I thought that maybe the living to whom I was to preach were inside.

I went inside and felt that I had come to a really awful place. The windows were black and dirty, covered with soot and cobwebs. It was impossible to see anything through them. When my eyes began to gradually make things out, I was startled to see that the room was filled with coffins. They were stacked one on top of the other, with only a narrow walkway in the middle.

I groped my way along this walkway, wondering whether or not there might be a back room with live people but I searched in vain. It was dark and a horrible deathly stench of decay hit my nostrils so that I didn't want to breathe. Accidentally, I got some decaying human flesh on my hands. At that, I turned back quickly and staggered out of this house of death.

I began to wipe my hands clean of the filth with my handkerchief and looked intently into the eyes of the angel. He had been following me the whole time. I said with vehemence, "This must be a mistake. No one can do anything here. The entire house is a horrible death chamber. I'm not going to go back in there."

The angel looked at me long and hard. Finally he said, "Do you think that God makes mistakes? Haven't you read in the Bible, "Neither say thou before the angel that it was an error."?

Until then I had never heard of such a passage. Later I found it in the fifth chapter of Ecclesiastes. The reference was to the making of promises:

> When thou vowest a vow unto God, defer not to pay it; for he hath no pleasure in fools: pay that which thou hast vowed. Better is it that thou shouldest not vow, than that thou shouldest vow and not pay. Suffer not thy mouth to cause thy flesh to sin; neither say thou before the angel, that it was an error: wherefore should God be angry at thy voice, and destroy the work of thine hands? (v.4-6).

God never makes mistakes -but people do.

The angel spoke again, "Now I ask you for the last time, do you or do you not want to fulfill the promise you made to God?"

I remembered very vividly the situation when I had been ordered to go to the battlefront and how God had solved that dilemma. It was very clear in my mind that I had promised to go to "God's battlefront" wherever that might be, to do whatever work He wanted me to do. There could certainly be no blessing for me if I didn't even attempt to obey God's will.

"I want to obey," I answered with a trembling voice.

"You must go back again into that house which you left a while ago," the angel said.

I remember how I gasped to get plenty of fresh air before I went in again. I thought to myself, *I don't have to look at all of that which is around me.* I closed my eyes and carefully walked into the middle of the synagogue and knelt there.

"I want to obey, Lord," I said. "Give me clear directions about what I can do in this chamber of death."

A Message to the People of Israel

A servant's obligation is to his master but not without rights. The servant has the right to clear instructions about his duties. This was my request as I knelt before my Lord. Then He gave me a remarkable message for the Jewish people:

> Despite the fact that you have rejected the Messiah Yeshua for the past two thousand years I still love you. God's grace is even now seeking you out. If you receive Him now then for you and for all of mankind there will be a new age. He will gather you to the land of your fathers and the kingdom of God will come.

This was easy for me to remember and recite out loud. When I finished, the Lord said, "Now you may get up and look around." When I opened my eyes I noticed a remarkable change. There was not a coffin in sight. The windows were crystal-clear in the first rays of the morning sun. Around me there were happy, blessed people dressed in pure white robes. They were thanking me for the message that I had given them.

"Don't thank me," I said. "This house has just experienced a wonderful miracle of God. When I first came in here I ran away horrified because there was nothing but death all around. Thank God because He has done a mighty miracle on your behalf!"

The angel came to my side and said, "Tell these people that they must wait a little while for this to happen." To me he said, "Prepare yourself for your calling in the midst of My people in Palestine, for the rest of your lifetime. That is the place for your life's work."

It was as if a curtain had been drawn. The angel disappeared and I awakened as if from a dream. This happened at Jyväskylä in the summer of 1944.

One should not blindly trust all visions, revelations or "callings." They need to be considered with care and studied in the light of God's Word. Having seen the vision I just described, I took my Bible and turned to

Ezekiel 37. I remembered that the prophet had had a similar manifestation from the Lord, in which God shows his servant the condition of the people of Israel. Ezekiel is shown a valley full of dead bones and then asked, "Can these bones live?" He is wise enough not to say, "No, it is quite impossible." He responds instead, "O Lord, You know."

The destiny of the people of Israel is not dependent upon man but rather on God. We are told of His plans in their regard in His Word. In Ezekiel 36, we read of God restoring the land, making it fertile and fruitful. In the next chapter God restores His people. First the dry bones come together and then God pours out His Spirit over them so that they begin to live again. In these chapters is found the powerful prophecy of events of this land's past and present history. Having been here for over fifty years I have had the privilege of seeing God gather His people to Israel.

What is yet lacking from the fulfillment of these prophecies is the pouring out of God's Spirit upon the dry bones. It is both the grace of God as well as our privilege to pray that they would come to life. We cannot save anyone nor can we give anyone God's Spirit, this is done only by God Himself. In the Scriptures we see that this is indeed His plan and His will. In Zechariah 12:10 the Lord says:

> And I will pour upon the house of David, and upon the inhabitants of Jerusalem, the spirit of grace and supplications: and they shall look upon me whom they have pierced, and they shall mourn for him, as one mourneth for his only son, and shall be in bitterness for him, as one that is in bitterness for his firstborn.

This prophecy has not yet come to pass, although it is sure to happen soon. It is a blessing and grace to be a messenger of the Lord at the exact place He needs me.

Chapter 5

Signs from Heaven

A Confirmation of the Calling

As the one in charge of the express office at Jyväskylä, my duties included receiving the bodies of the war victims that were on their way to central Finland. I had to report the names of the victims to a military chaplain and he in turn would notify the relatives.

For several years I was a friend of one of these chaplains, the Reverend Vilho Rantanen, pastor of the Free Church. One day after taking care of "business" with the reverend I told him my personal news, that I would not be in my position much longer because the Lord had called me to work among the Jews in Palestine.

There was silence at the other end of the line. Then he said, "Look, brother, I know that you are overburdened and that you haven't had a vacation for a long time. You ought to see a doctor and then take some time off."

"This is no business for a doctor," I replied. "This is a calling from God."

Many years later when Rantanen came on a "Holy Land tour," he came to see his old friend now in Tiberias. Already as he climbed the steps to our home he asked forgiveness for not understanding and for not responding to my calling in the right way right from the beginning. Now he understood and rejoiced with me.

The truth is, his reaction had not been an exception to that of my other friends and family. Not many were able to understand my calling, including my relatives. The only one who encouraged me was the old veteran pastor of the Jyväskylä Pentecostal Church, Akseli Puhakainen. His comment was: "If God has called you, He has the power to care for you and your family. Go in the Name of Jesus!" And he gave me his blessing.

God confirmed His calling to me in various ways. On one such occasion, I had a kind of "face-to-face" with Him. Ezekiel relates a similar experience. When he saw God sitting on His throne he fell on his face due to the bright glory emanating from Him. God then gave him a mission among His people.

The Lord told me, "Listen, Kaarlo! You have made a promise to me and the time has now come to fulfill it."

Then he showed me a huge map of Palestine. Pointing to the Upper Galilee area, the Sea of Galilee in particular, He said, "This area has been empty and deserted for a long time but soon I will have my people return there. I want to establish a new 'station' on the shores of the Sea and I appoint you the 'stationmaster' of that 'station' for the rest of your life."

"But Lord," I protested. "I don't know Hebrew and not even much English. Maybe You could find a wiser man in my place. That post is in a foreign country and I wouldn't be able to take care of it anyway."

"Be faithful and listen obediently," the Lord replied. "I will help you in everything. This is the place intended for you."

One morning in 1944 I was awakened and I heard a clear voice that said, "You will soon get to prepare for the work to which you are called. Be ready!"

I thought to myself, *What does this 'soon' mean? Is it a matter of years or days?* In any case, I wrote up my resignation so that I could send it as soon as it became necessary. I felt like a bird on a branch, ready to fly.

In October of that same year, a telegram arrived:

> Truce with Soviet Union. Karelia has surrendered. How many Ingrian railroad employees can be assigned to the Jyväskylä station?

I immediately took my resignation papers to the stationmaster's office, requesting to be released from my position as soon as possible.

On 15 October 1944 an inventory was made of the cash on hand (which amounted to several million marks) and I was accorded an honorable discharge from my position with the state railroad.

A Land Deal

Evangelist Kerttu Siikala came from Larsmo to Jyväskylä. She explained that the construction of homes for those headed overseas was to be started there soon, specifically for all those called to Christian service in a foreign country.

When I heard this news, I left at once for Larsmo. There I helped the construction team in the building project while at the same time studying for my future work. When the houses were finished, my family came as well and we lived there for two years, from 1945 to 1947.

We still had the country farm at Kintaus. Our neighbor, a farmer named Rajala, had many children. He came over to chat and explained that it wasn't possible to make a living on his small farm because there wasn't enough cow pasture. "Would you sell me a part of your land," he asked, "so that I could make a suitable farm out of my small one?" I sold him a seventeen-hectare plot and he was very pleased.

Then a certain Karelian man came to see me with a different kind of problem. "I was given some land at Muurame as remuneration for that which I lost in Karelia. There isn't even a lake nearby. You have a nice place here on the lakeshore. Is there any chance of us trading farms?" I agreed and so we made a deal. In exchange, we received a fifty-six-hectare farm of which sixteen hectares were in cultivation. The Karelian was delighted with our smaller farm endowed with a lakeshore and forest.

And so I killed three, not two, "birds with one stone." We still had a farm (a large one with valuable forest), Rajala was happy to have an extension to his property and the evacuated Karelian got a farm to his liking!

While I was studying at Larsmo, I got a call to meet with the Land Management Council. They asked me if it was true that I was planning on going overseas. I answered in the affirmative.

"How long do you plan to stay there?" the chairman asked.

"For the rest of my life," I replied.

"Is that so? What about your family? Do you have a family?"

"A wife and four children."

"Will they stay to take care of the farm when you leave?"

"They wouldn't stay here," I answered. "They will come later, as soon as they can."

"We need land now for the Karelians. You won't receive permission to leave the country as long you own a large plot of land."

"Let's clear this up as soon as possible then," I replied.

I was asked to leave the room for a few minutes. When I returned they said: "You can sell your farm voluntarily to the state if you wish, but to tell you the truth, you won't receive payment for it for at least ten years. We are fixing the price of your farm at 200,000 Finnish marks (2,000 FIM in 1987). Here is the contract. Simply sign your name!"

I already had Maire's authorization just in case it would be necessary and so with a few strokes of a pen the entire 56 hectares (112 acres) was sold.

The Lord gave me great inner joy and peace in this matter. I shook hands with the land surveyor, thanked him and wished him God's blessing in his task of acquiring farms for the Karelian people.

He looked at me in amazement and said, "It's most unusual for someone to leave like this. Usually landowners leave the Board Meeting swearing as they go."

But I was able to experience in a marvelous way the truth of Hebrews 10:34: *..took joyfully the spoiling of your goods, knowing in yourselves that ye have in heaven a better and an enduring substance.* This shows the grace and faithfulness of the Lord. And it has lasted and will last forever.

The chairman of the Land Management Council wrote about our case to the Ministry of Finance. As a result, we received the following letter:

> Your case appears to be an exception. It has been recommended that you be paid at least a part of the purchase price now in cash. You will be receiving 70,000 marks immediately even though the payment should not be made until ten years from now.

In this way the Lord provided us with money to travel to Israel. The rest was eaten by inflation.

A Step Forward

In 1946 I felt certain that it was time to move onward. One of the first Christian conferences after the war was to be held in Sweden. Arne Lyman, of the Larsmo community where we lived asked if I would like to go there with him.

"Gladly," I replied.

"Good. You will need an invitation from Sweden before you can leave the country," he said, and without further hesitation, wrote to the conference organizers with the request. The invitation arrived. I still needed a permit to leave which certified that there was no obstacle to my leaving the country -valid for one month only. Then of course the visa to Sweden, not to speak of a passport!

We were living in critical times, the "Leino times" as they were called, named after the Interior Minister. The situation in Finland was not yet stabilized. Many people wanted to leave but permission was refused.

I received a week's visa! The question remained, "How would my trip be funded?" I did not have a single mark for travel costs and besides, Finnish money was not acceptable in Sweden in those days. The Swedish Bank would not exchange Finnish money and I didn't even have any Swedish coins. I had to leave on my journey fully trusting in God's mercy and guidance without cash in my pocket or plans in my head! The ticket I purchased from Finland was one-way only. But the way was clear!

I was housed with someone from outside of Scandinavia. When I introduced myself, he embraced me, kissed both of my cheeks and joyfully asked, "Are you really a Finn?"

"Yes," I replied.

"I am the pastor of Madrid's only evangelical congregation," he continued. "During the war when you had very hard times in Finland, we in Madrid prayed much on behalf of your country and its people. You are the first Finn that I've ever seen and that is why I wanted to greet you so lovingly."

"I have one question," he continued. "When we prayed so often in our congregation on your behalf, sometimes I would wake up even during the night and pray in tongues. I suspect that in that period when you in Finland were in such difficulties, I prayed even in my sleep for God's mercy on your small country. In my prayers one word was repeated again and again. I've asked many people what this word means but no one so far has been able to explain it to me. So I'm asking you: What does the word *Jumala* mean and what language is it from?"

"Well, that is plainly Finnish and it means God," I answered. "It seems that when you spoke in tongues through the power of the Holy Spirit, God allowed you to speak in the tongue of the nation on whose behalf you were praying."

This brother and I became good friends and we corresponded for several years. I suspect he has by now gone to be with the Lord.

A Remarkable Dream

When I arrived in Sweden, I had great hopes. It seemed to be a nation of peace, saved from the horrors and ravages of war. At Kaggeholm, the Pentecostals had a training center for overseas Christian workers where the teachers spoke English. I went to see Lewi Pethrus to ask him whether they would take me as a student in this Bible school.

"Where are you headed?" he asked.

"To Palestine, to work among the Jews," I answered.

During the first few minutes of our conversation, he had appeared to be rather encouraging but when he heard "Palestine" and "Jews," I sensed an immediate roadblock.

"Jews don't need anything and there is nothing that can be done in Palestine. They have plenty of Christians, ministers and churches. Nothing can be done there. Only when God's appointed time comes will He save them as a nation -in one day- according to the Scriptures."

As gifted and as Spirit-filled as this man of God was, he had no vision for the work that needed to be done among the Israeli people, not that anyone else did either, at the time!

Nevertheless, I went to see the secretary of the overseas department, Nystrom of the local Philadelphia-church congregation. He was an experienced man in his field. I asked him whether they had any workers in the Middle East and whether they had any contacts in this area to which I felt called by God.

"We have none," he replied, "and besides, Christians are not needed there. War is going to break out and God will surely take care of their affairs when His time comes. England has been active in that part of the world. It's absolutely useless to hustle and bustle in an attempt to do something in that land in these times."

We reached the last evening meeting of the conference. All present, including candidates such as myself, were asked to come up onto the platform. Each one spoke about his own place of calling, where he had been and where he was planning to go.

There was much rejoicing and thanking the Lord, everyone feeling blessed. But I left weeping from that last meeting. Deeply saddened I went to my room and knelt before the Lord. With a lump in my throat, I poured out my disappointment to God: "Lord, why is it that these great spiritual leaders don't understand at all the need for Your work among the Jewish people? In Your mercy, let me now see the situation as it really is. If my calling is still valid as far as You are concerned, then show me whether it is worthwhile for me to continue or whether I should return to Finland. I need clear confirmation of the calling You have given me, even though You have done this many times in the past. Now I need it again since there is so much opposition from spiritual leaders."

After praying, I went to sleep and the Lord gave me a remarkable dream. It was a beautiful summer day at a lovely beach. People were sun tanning and children were splashing in the water. But farther away, beyond the peaceful shore of the sea, there seemed to be a violent storm raging. A large ocean-liner anchored there was being hastily readied for departure.

Well, what do you know? I thought to myself. *With that ship one could get to one's destination far beyond the seas!* But when I approached it, I noticed to my great dismay that the captain was Lewi Pethrus and that the first mate was secretary Nystrom!

Along with the others, my family and I were trying to board the ship. We came on deck and waited for the time of departure. At last the ship was ready and the order was heard, "Raise the anchors! We are leaving."

I was sure that we were now leaving on that long voyage for which we had been preparing ourselves. But to my great surprise, the ship turned along the shallow, sandy shoreline. The water was so clear that I could see all the way to the bottom. This alarmed me. "For goodness' sake," I said, "they're going to run the ship aground! With a vessel like this, one doesn't sail right along the shoreline!"

Some distance from the ship I could make out seaweed on the seabottom where a school of fish were spawning. These were clearly visible through the water.

When the ship's captain saw the fish, he gave the order, "Drop the anchors! We will now start fishing!"

The large ocean-liner stopped and the anchors were dropped. The lifeboats were lowered and the fishing began. When I saw this, I went straight to the Captain and asked him, "Excuse me, Captain, but how long do you intend to fish?"

"What do you mean? There are fish here. There is no way we are going anywhere from this place! Why did you force your way on this ship if you didn't want to fish? We are not moving."

And so I left the captain and went to the stern of the ship to pray. *Oh Heavenly Father! Forgive me! We have boarded the wrong ship! This one is going nowhere. These people are fishing in the seaweed. Now I need your advice.*

I had scarcely finished that prayer when an angel approached me. He had in his hand something like a child's toy ship, perhaps a little over a meter in length and twenty to thirty centimeters wide. He held it out to me and said, "Here is your means of travel! It's what you asked for, isn't it?"

I took a long look at this model of a ship and thought, *This is certainly a tiny ship! How can it last? My whole family can hardly fit into that.*

The angel guessed my thoughts and said: "You're likely thinking that this ship is so small that it won't carry anything. But notice one thing. It is God's gift to you, along with a God-given guarantee. It won't sink even in the worst of storms. Whatever cargo you put in it, it will carry it all. Will this do for you?" the angel asked.

"Yes, it will do! Thank you very much," I replied. But the ship wasn't completely finished. It didn't have a deck.

"But the deck is missing," I told the angel. "The ship isn't quite ready yet."

"God doesn't give something completely finished. You have to build a deck for it yourself."

"But we are already en route. Our home has been emptied out and all our things are packed...."

At that point the angel interrupted me and said, "But you have Mirja's mattress, don't you?" Our youngest child's special mattress, which was occasionally used, we now stuffed into the space where the deck should have been, and somehow the mattress filled that space.

I took the "ship" under my arm, found the rope ladder of the ocean-liner and climbed down to the level of the sea and set my own ship on the waves. At first I was afraid that it might sink under my weight, but it didn't! Then Maire and the children came on board as well. I remember clearly that I pushed away from the large ocean-liner that was like an imposing brick house next to our ship. I pushed hard until we were at a good distance from it.

My last words at the end of the dream: "Thanks be to God that we can travel with our own ship!"

I have often recalled this remarkable dream and wondered about that mattress of Mirja's. My conclusion is that it could not be anything but a child-like faith in God. The Scriptures say that without faith it is impossible to please God. Once we start out on God's "road" we must believe what He says and act accordingly, no matter how illogical His directions may seem to us. Only through submission and obedience will the Lord bless us and help us.

The Little Ship Sails

Back at the conference, when morning arrived, Nyman said to me, "You will of course soon be returning to Finland."

"No I won't because I don't yet have a return ticket!" I answered.

"Do you have any friends here?" he asked. "Do you have any money?"

"No. Neither friends nor money." I replied.

"Well where will you stay?" he continued to inquire.

"I can't answer that yet, God will probably reveal it to me at the right time."

We bade each other farewell. He returned to Finland and I stayed to await the time when that little ship would sail.

We were still in the conference grounds when a loud voice cried over the loudspeaker: "Attention, attention! This is the last announcement before the loudspeaker system is dismantled. Is there anyone here who could be an interpreter for the Ingrian refugees? If so, please come to the office at once. The Ingrian Embassy is looking for you."

Thousands of former Ingrians had come to Sweden. They didn't understand Swedish and the Swedes didn't know Finnish. They wanted to attend religious meetings but they lacked an interpreter who could translate the Swedish speeches into Finnish.

I went to the office and told them that I had the time and was available to serve as their interpreter. There I met several of the Ingrian Christian leaders, among them Teppo Telkkinen. They were so grateful that they embraced me, exclaiming, "Thank God we found someone who can help us!" I could do it since as a government employee in Finland I had had to learn Swedish. So my bilingualism was a help to me in my state of distress and to the refugees in theirs!

From that moment, the "little ship" began to sail past the school of fish.

By the following evening we were in Gothenburg. The next day there was to be a large Ingrian summer festival near the city. I was able to serve as an interpreter there and even to speak a little myself. That entire summer of 1946 was a remarkable and blessed time as I worked among the refugees. It was from among this group that our oldest son Olavi later found his wife Ester.

Chapter 6

Encouragement in Trials

A Brother with a Similar Calling

That same summer I met a Swedish brother who had a burden on his heart to work among the Jewish refugees in Sweden. During the war, twenty to thirty thousand Jews had come there to escape persecution by Hitler.

He presented the matter to Lewi Pethrus and told him that he had ten to fifteen thousand crowns in savings that he was willing to give towards the printing of Bibles to the Jews in various languages.

Pethrus answered that God would surely take care of that matter Himself and that we needn't do this kind of work. Such a task should not be our concern at all. He did not by any means want to take part in an endeavor "of this kind."

This Swedish brother told me with a tearful voice about this conversation and of the work that he then began to do on his own initiative. He had the Evangeliipress in Orebro print New Testaments. Later on, I received news of this brother through Ingemar Hallzon, a mutual colleague in matters concerning Bible publishing.

I no longer recall his name but I know that for many, many years he worked in Sweden on behalf of Jewish refugees. I believe that his work was precious in the sight of God.

God Sees my Need

Fall was approaching when I noticed a newspaper advertisement for the Falkoping Park English-language Bible school. It was a two-month course costing one hundred and fifty crowns a month, all expenses included. I wanted very much to attend but of course I had no money to pay for it. At the time I was living at Molnlyck with the Telkkinens. On Sunday, the day before the course was to begin, I left early to take a walk in a nearby forest, to call on the Lord, that He might from somewhere give me the money for the course fees.

I was absorbed in the tranquility of the woods when suddenly I heard someone calling my name.

I finally answered and began walking toward the voice calling. A certain Ingrian sister came toward me and said, "I have been saving money to buy a winter coat but the Lord told me that I can still get by with my old one. He said, *Take the money quickly to Kaarlo! He needs it.*"

"I thought I had left early enough this morning to get here but you had already gone. There was nothing left to do but to follow you and call out your name."

She reached out to give me an envelope and when I opened it, I saw that it contained exactly one hundred and fifty crowns, the fee for the first month of the Bible-study course!

"I don't know why you need this money," she said.

"I know very well," I replied. "Tomorrow is the first day of a Bible course at Falkoping. I was just now praying for the money so that I could attend. Thank you for obeying His voice!"

Once again, I had reason to thank the Lord for taking such good care of me. But it was a two-month course. When the first month was nearing its end, I became doubtful. *Where could I possibly get the money to pay the second month's fee?* And it would not be right to go into debt.

On the last morning of the last day of the month, I put the Lord to the test. I said to Him: "If in Your mercy You will permit me to continue these studies for the second month, then I ask You for the sign that at tonight's meeting the song which begins with the words, *Pour out, Lord, Your Spirit again...* will be sung. It will be a sign that You will allow me to continue another month and that You will provide the money. If we don't sing it, then it will be a sign that I must go to work and drop out of the course."

At the meeting, the usual program was followed but my song was not sung. So sadly, I thought, *How unfortunate, tomorrow I will have to go find work somewhere.*

Just as the people were leaving, one of the sisters said, "Listen, friends! Do you know the song, *Pour out, Lord, Your Spirit again...*?" We sang the song. This was a powerful answer to my prayer and I had ample reason to give thanks for this was the very song of which I had spoken to the Lord.

Afterwards, I went to see the sister and asked her, "What on earth made you think of this song and especially at the very end?!"

"I don't know. During the whole meeting I had a powerful urge to suggest that song but I stubbornly resisted. I told the Lord, 'I will not suggest it! I don't even know it. I can't remember ever having sung it myself'. And even at the end, I wouldn't have suggested it, but then the Lord insisted and said, *If you don't suggest the song you will be committing a great sin!* Then I just <u>had</u> to obey," the sister said.

"Thank God that you obeyed Him!"

I went to pick up my mail. I just knew that the Lord would help me in this crisis. Indeed He did: There was a registered letter for me containing two hundred crowns. This sufficed for my needs until the end of the course.

The course was excellent, with much variety. Many of the teachers were old veterans of the Pentecostal revival, among them Paul Ongman, well known by Swedish believers. An English couple gave good Bible studies. These were a great blessing and very necessary for my preparation. I was much in need of the training that I received there for my future work. At the same course there were about twenty candidates ready for departure to their respective places of calling.

By the end of the term, winter was beginning. I wanted very much to get to England. During the summer conference, I had met Donald Gee, a respected Bible teacher who had been in Finland many times at the

Pentecostal Bible school. At the conference I had asked him if he could help me get into a Bible school in England. He answered with, "I'll see what I can do. We'll talk about it again tomorrow."

I assume that in the meantime he consulted with Lewi Pethrus because when I met him again he said, "There is no way that we can help you. Besides, you are on your way to Palestine, where workers are not needed."

A third blind one, I thought. It is remarkable to note that "big trees cast big shadows." Even Donald Gee didn't understand anything about the Lord's work among the Jews.

Since this was the state of affairs I could do nothing but speak to the Lord about it. "Now what should I do," I asked Him. "In one way or another I should get to England but I don't have any money nor do I see any possibilities opening up!"

An Open Door to England

One day in October of 1946, I received a remarkable letter from England. It was from the Worldwide Evangelical Crusade, otherwise known as WEC, founded by C.T. Studd. The Executive Secretary, N.P. Grubb wrote in the letter:

> We have heard that you are trying to get to Palestine to work among the Jews. We want to help you and we offer you expense-free living here in our London Center. You are welcome whenever it is convenient for you to come and your stay here will cost you nothing.

This letter was a powerful answer to my prayer. I took the letter with me to the English Embassy at Gothenburg and received a visa for England. Some friends gave me enough money to buy a ticket for a ship going to England.

I heard that there was a shortage in England of all stationery products. I collected some supplies from different places and so as I was boarding the ship, I had all sorts of bundles dangling from my arms. The same Swedish brother who had earlier sent me two hundred crowns again happened to meet me. When he saw the many packages, he asked me in amazement, "Don't you have a suitcase!?"

"No, such things were not made in Finland during the war."

"You are not to go to England like that!" He said. "There is a brother who owns a luggage shop not far from here. We'll go there right now!"

We got the best and most elegant suitcase in the shop. I even got a second one, larger but more ordinary looking. With the help of a Swedish sister who was there in the shop, I quickly packed my belongings. I put my clothes and the more valuable things into the fancy suitcase. When we finished packing, I heard an inner voice saying, "Now hurry, exchange the contents of these two pieces of luggage. Put your books, notebooks and the heavier things into the fancy suitcase, and into that ordinary-looking trunk put your clothes and whatever else is of value."

The sister naturally asked with surprise, "Why? Why do you have to exchange those things?"

"I don't know," I answered, "but it is best to obey."

At customs they asked me, "Do you have Swedish money? You cannot take it out of the country."

"Let's see how much there is," I said, and found two crowns in my wallet. "Is this too much?!" I asked with a laugh. I was leaving the country with practically nothing, with the customs official staring at me, likely thinking, *Is this a fool or is he lying*?

Upon arrival in London, two porters rushed to my side and grabbed my heavy luggage. Each one of them got a crown and so I was left penniless right then and there.

I found myself at Victoria Station in London without any money. I had heard that the English police were very friendly and that one could ask them for advice and get help. So I went to an officer standing nearby, showed him the letter I had received from London and with poor English asked for directions to the organization mentioned in the letter.

He looked questioningly at my suitcases and said, "It's at least ten miles from here. A newcomer like you will never get there with that luggage. They should come to get you."

Then the same polite police officer phoned the WEC office and told them that there was a newcomer that they should come to fetch at the station. It was perhaps an hour later when someone emerged from the subway entrance and asked, "Are you Charles from Finland?"

"Yes!" I answered.

He glanced at my luggage and said, "We can't take such heavy luggage on the subway. Let's have them come by train."

"You know what is best," I replied in agreement.

The next morning my trunk arrived but the fancy suitcase did not.

What would have happened if I hadn't obeyed the inner voice I heard in Gothenburg? Clothing was rationed at the time and one couldn't get ration cards for clothes in a foreign country. I thanked the Lord that I had sense enough to obey even in small matters.

The next day I was notified by the station that my suitcase had been found, broken open. They asked me to see whether anything was missing.

It had contained Finnish and English books, notebooks and other heavy articles. The thief must have been very disappointed with the contents of the suitcase! The Railroad Company paid my claim for the broken locks and for the few missing articles.

Chapter 7

England

Peeling Potatoes

My life in London began pleasantly. I was informed that as promised, everything was free. The only expectation was that the students help with the housekeeping chores: "At the moment, however, all of the men's jobs have been assigned. You won't be insulted will you, if you were to give a little help to the women in the kitchen? They need someone to peel potatoes."

"One can surely learn to do that," I answered and went at once to the kitchen.

The English never boil unpeeled potatoes. Even if there is a shortage of them, they are always peeled. The WEC School had between fifty and sixty people so it took a couple of hours to peel enough potatoes for the whole group.

Some time later, more kitchen help arrived. I then shared the task with a student from Switzerland named Henri. He didn't peel very long before he wrote home for a potato-peeling machine. We were instantly promoted from peelers to machine-operators and during the last part of our stay, the machine did our hard work!

England

Life at WEC was constructive in every way. We studied hard and therefore learned a lot. We were informed of the current situations in the countries of our destination, on behalf of which we prayed a great deal. We ourselves were ready to be used by the Lord whenever doors would open up for us.

Henri was my roommate. One day he asked me for advice, saying, "Listen, Charles! I've become quite fond of that Agnes, who works in the kitchen.... What do you think? Do I dare ask her to marry me?"

"That's a very important and delicate matter," I replied. "Let's take this to the Lord. Then do as He leads you."

Together we prayed about this question. Henri received assurance in his heart that this was God's will and who knows, perhaps some encouragement from Agnes as well, so he finally dared to tell her of his love.

Thus they became an engaged couple at the college. After the wedding, Henri received a call to Indonesia. Agnes stood by her husband, ready to share with him the joys and sorrows of that field.

"How awful," some reacted, hearing about Indonesia. "The natives there are so disgusted with the Whites, you'll never leave there alive. An uprising is developing and war is imminent. There are even cannibals among them. Dear friends, don't even attempt to go there! There are other places in this world...."

Henri and Agnes left for Indonesia at the same time I did for Palestine. They labored there faithfully day after day. War and riots did break out as they had been warned. Indonesia broke loose from Dutch rule. It gained independence and now it is perhaps the fifth largest country in the world with a population of one hundred and thirty million, most of whom are Muslims.

But when the country was on the brink of anarchy, God sent a powerful revival that changed everything. Henri and Agnes were pioneer Christian workers in the land, and they were able to rejoice in those powerful acts of God seen in Indonesia during this time. The revival in Indonesia continues still.

A Pleasant Surprise

While I was in London, I needed a typewriter but after the war they were very hard to get. Even the rejected ones were salvaged for use. A decent typewriter was seldom to be seen.

One day as an English brother and I were reading the Scriptures, we came across the verse, "If two of you shall agree on earth as touching any thing that they shall ask, it shall be done for them of my Father which is in heaven" (Matthew 18:19).

"Do you believe this to be true?" I inquired of my brother.

"Of course it is because it's in the Bible," he answered.

"Well I need a typewriter. Would you agree to join me in asking the Lord for one and to have it brought to me here in England?" He agreed with me in prayer and I forgot about the whole thing.

Then a letter came from Sanfrid Mattson announcing that he and his wife were coming to London. I went to meet them at the station. He was carrying a large case and even before we properly greeted each other, he shouted, "Look at this, Kaarlo! The Lord sent you a typewriter, it's in this case!"

A month had passed since our prayer.

"One of your many friends sent it for you to Larsmo and so we brought it with us."

I noticed a note attached to the case. It read: "A gift from the Lord for the use of the Lord."

Later, when I received a new and better typewriter, I gave the old one to a handicapped Messianic believer in Eilat.

"To Obey is Better than Sacrifice"

Urgent word was brought to me. "Listen, Charles! There is a critical situation in Palestine just now. It looks as if a serious war is about to begin.

Don't even think of going there yet, good friend. Stay here and wait for things to clear up."

Then new possibilities were brought to my attention: "Charles! Here is your great opportunity! The BBC, England's national radio network is looking for an announcer to translate the English news into Finnish. They are to begin a ten to fifteen-minute Finnish-language program to be broadcast three times a week. Sounds like a fine career for you!" Such a person had long been sought. In 1946-1947 there were very few Finns in England.

The suggestion-makers continued, "We know the directors at the BBC. You can get the job right now! And soon the whole of Finland will be hearing your voice -those who know you as well as those who don't!"

"Listen and I'll tell you what I think of this suggestion," I answered. "This idea is nothing more than a detour arranged by the devil and I'm not going to take it! The Lord has never called me to read the often-biased reports of the BBC. I must get to Palestine, is that clear? It is there that I have promised the Lord I would go, no matter what the situation, war or peace. I must move on."

I went to the WEC treasurer, retired Colonel Mandro married to the daughter of C.T. Studd, the founder of the school. I told him of my plans.

"What kind of visa do you want?" he asked.

"I want a permanent immigrant visa to Palestine for myself, my wife and my children. I have a life-long call to be there and I have promised it to the Lord."

"Excellent! Write down the names of all the members of your family along with their birth dates," the colonel said. "The governor general of Palestine is one of my former officer-friends. I will write to him about your situation. We'll see what kind of reply we get from him."

A month later, the colonel called me to his office and said, "Look Charles, the answer has arrived." The governor general's letter read:

> Upon your request and the recommendation received we have granted the Finnish Christian Kaarlo Olavi Syväntö and his entire family a permanent, life-long visa to Palestine.

Official seals and signatures embellished the letter.

What a powerful answer to prayer!

Sewing Supplies

Another happy incident took place when Anna-Liisa and Sanfrid Mattson were in London on their way to Ethiopia. A certain Christian lady invited the three of us for Sunday lunch. The morning of that day we were to be at the Baptist church worship service.

In my quarters, as I was getting ready, I noticed that one of the buttons on my suit jacket was about to drop off. After fixing the problem, a rather long strand of black thread was left in the eye of the needle. I was about to set it aside (men generally don't carry such items with them!) when I clearly heard the Lord say, "Do not put away that needle and thread. Take them with you!"

I must be losing my mind, I thought. *What in the world would I do with a needle and thread? Surely the buttons on my jacket will stay on, especially since I've just checked them!*

I stuck the needle and thread onto a curtain as I had seen some women do. Then I had a start when I heard the Lord say, "Don't you want to obey me even in little things?"

"I do, Lord! Forgive me!"

I took the needle again and carefully wrapped it with the thread onto a piece of paper that I put into a compartment of my wallet. Only then did I have a clear conscience.

The Mattsons and I met at the Baptist Church. Anna-Liisa sat between Sanfrid and myself. She was wearing a formal black dress and black hose to match. Somehow, her stocking caught onto something on the edge of the pew and a snapping sound announced that there was a tear. True enough, a line of skin was visible from the knee down.

Crestfallen, Anna-Liisa began to dig into her handbag and having groped around for a while, she whispered, "How awful! I don't have a needle and black thread with me."

Turning to me she said, "I would truly be grateful and thank the Lord if I only had a needle and a bit of black thread with me. Look what happened. How can I go to the luncheon like this? Everyone will notice and besides, it's Sunday. Where on earth could I get a needle and thread now?"

"Here you are," I said, rather reluctantly taking out my wallet and pulling out the sewing supplies. "Now you can be grateful and thank the Lord," I told her with a chuckle. Anna-Liisa quickly repaired the stocking. She was so very thankful. It was the one and only time that I have had a needle and some black thread in my possession at a religious meeting!

I have often reminisced about my stay in London. Earlier, I had regretted that Donald Gee did not see fit to help me get into his Bible school. I had actually been very disappointed about it. With time, however, I have come to realize that his refusal was part of God's plan. If I had been there I would never have been able to get a permanent visa to Palestine. The Lord directed my life along a "higher route." He led me along pioneering paths that He knew I would be able to take.

The Bible assures us that "all things work together for good to them that love God" (Romans 8:28). This is truly the case in my experience. Mysterious are His ways and His direction!

Chapter 8

Destination Palestine

The Lord my Provider

I was penniless. The ticket to Palestine would cost something. I told the Lord although He knew without my reminding Him that I needed money.

In Sweden, there is a publishing company called Evangeliipress, founded by Florentius Hallzon. He was a warm-hearted Christian and a great friend of the Jews. His well-known Christian newspaper *Hemmets Van* is read even in Finland. Currently his sons continue their father's work.

Hallzon came to London for a visit and I was his guide for the week. By then I knew my way around the city, as I had been there already eight months. When we were about to part, he said, "So you did get that visa to Palestine, didn't you? We have been printing the Gospels for the Scripture Gift Mission but they cannot send money out of England even in order to pay their bill due to the strict regulations. You need money as you are leaving for Palestine, do you not? I will have them pay you the amount they owe me."

We went immediately to the SCM office and they gave me their debt to the Evangeliipress, a total of between seventy and eighty pounds. "Here is money for the trip to Palestine," Hallzon said with a smile. And so we parted.

Another miraculous answer to prayer!

Hurdles to Overcome

I went to the travel agency to ask about a ticket to Palestine. The reply was: "Impossible! The government has bought up all ship tickets for the next two years for transporting soldiers and evacuees. Palestine is on the brink of war and English citizens are being brought back. Soldiers are sent to replace them. It is not possible!"

That seemed to be the end of it.

As I was making my exit from the travel agency, I said, "Listen, Lord. What can I do now since they said it is impossible to get on a ship? You gave me a visa and travel money. Please give me the wisdom to know what to do. Once again this must be the devil at work. He is trying to prevent my journey."

The Lord replied: "Egypt is a colony of England. Ships travel via the Suez Canal to India. In the near future, a ship is leaving England for India on this route. Go back to the agency and ask them for a ticket on a ship bound for India!"

So I went back and asked, "Is a ship leaving here in the near future for India?"

"Yes, in a week's time the Ascania, a luxury steamship, is heading for India."

"Have all the berths been reserved?" I asked.

"Oh no, there is room for any number of people," the agent answered.

"Good! Reserve a place for me as far as Port Said," I announced, and paid the forty pounds for my ticket.

Then I phoned the Egyptian Embassy to ask for a transit visa from Egypt to Palestine.

"Fine, that is easily arranged. It will take less than ten minutes. You may retrieve it shortly before your departure," I was assured.

Everything seemed to be in order. I had only to catch the train to the Liverpool harbor. Two hours before the train's departure I went to the Egyptian Embassy, showed my passport and said, "I came to get that transit visa for Egypt that I called about earlier."

The officials stared at me rather irately and the one who handled my passport was downright rude. He hardly glanced at it and threw it back at me from the window so that it fell to the floor. It was as if the devil himself were at the window jeering at me. "We're not giving you any such visa! We don't know who may have promised you one over the telephone. You will never get to Palestine via Egypt. Take whatever other route you can find."

I picked up the passport from the floor and considered a plan of action. The Lord had now provided me with an immigrant visa, travel money as well as a reservation on the ship. It was clear: The enemy of my soul was opposing my trip. The Bible says, "Resist the devil, and he will flee from you" (James 4:7). *Nothing except a strong counter-attack will help at this point*, I thought.

With my passport in hand, I returned to the window and said, "I want to see the chief consul himself. Immediately." When he came, I demanded an answer. "What do you mean by denying me a transit visa for Egypt? It was promised me but these gentlemen refuse to provide it. My train is leaving within two hours and if I lose my immigrant visa and my reservation on board the ship, you will suffer the consequences. I will not accept any word-of-mouth explanations. I want the reason for this in writing, with the official's signature. Has war broken out between Egypt and Finland since a Finnish citizen isn't allowed a transit visa? If you deny me this visa, I will go directly to the Finnish Embassy and demand through them, an explanation from you. Now do I get a visa or not?"

The consul looked sober. Suddenly he said, "Wait a moment!" He spoke discreetly with the other officials and then turning to me said, "Forgive me sir! There has been a serious error. Please come to my office."

He opened the door for me with courtesy. As he offered me a seat he asked, "Where is your passport?"

Without further deliberation, he wrote on it the necessary entries, stamped it and said, "Here you are. Have a good trip!"

I still have that passport.

At Port Said there is an organization that was established by Swedish-Finns. I wired them from the ship, told them I was coming and asked them to send someone to meet me at the harbor. I had heard horror stories about that city, where thieves rob travelers right in the port.

When we were almost there, I received word from the organization. They had paid a man to come meet me. Indeed, when we arrived, an African of enormous size, bigger than any man I had ever seen, was waiting for me. This "giant" took care of collecting my many pieces of luggage. I had come to stay permanently in Palestine and therefore brought a fair number of things with me.

The harbor was teeming with people. Many porters would have wanted to carry my belongings but all of them seemed to be afraid of the "giant." He chased away those who had no business being there. Then he spoke to me in broken English. I understood that he was inquiring if I had twelve pieces of luggage.

"Yes," I replied.

The man found a taxi, loaded it with my belongings and off we went. The next day I continued the journey, once again accompanied by the same man. In London I had purchased a train ticket from Kantara to Lod and so the following day, in July of 1947, I reached my destination: The Promised Land.

My First Special Permit

I came into contact with the BEM, an American Christian organization in Jerusalem. Miss Raedford, one of their veteran workers, kindly took me in.

Jerusalem at the time was divided into security zones, with English soldiers stationed at their borders. When I wanted to go to the Bible shop, I discovered that it was located in a zone I was not allowed to enter without a special permit. Because I tend to face problems "head on" - particularly when these are related to the Lord's work- I wrote a letter to the military commander in Jerusalem. I explained to him that I had received a life-long visa as a Christian worker in Palestine. Furthermore, I was absolutely astonished that I was not allowed to go to the city's Bible shop. Hence my request for a permit to travel without restrictions in all zones of Jerusalem.

In reply I received a friendly letter with a promise to take care of the matter. I was simply asked to send three or four photographs of myself.

A week later, the permit arrived! I showed it to a Swedish acquaintance and colleague and she could not hide her amazement. "You Finns sure know how to take care of business, don't you! I have never seen such a permit, much less dared to ask for one!" she exclaimed.

A House in the Galilee

Some time later, the Lord led me to the northern part of the country, to the Galilee. In a city called Safed, the Scottish Mission had a fine house that had hardly been used for a long time. I heard that they would be glad to rent part of it and because I was expecting the arrival of my family, I went to take a look at it.

In the house there lived a Messianic family. He was very pleased that someone else with the same mission would join him. So I rented two rooms and a kitchen, planning to have my family join us by Christmas 1947.

Safed is a beautiful city. It is located on a high mountain from which there is an excellent view in every direction, including the Sea of Galilee.

November 1947

However, my good intentions remained only good intentions. God's "clock" which in regard to the Jews had seemingly stopped for nearly two thousand years, suddenly began to chime once again.

My generation will remember 29 November 1947, when in Great Britain partition was the subject of discussion. It was then that the Jews were granted the permission to establish their own state. This decision was a miracle, especially because the Soviet Union and the United States were agreed on the matter and actually gave their mutual support to the decision.

The following night, tumultuous clamor rang out in the streets of Safed. Wondering what was going on, I went outside. A young girl ran up to me and with a smile, pinned a slip of paper on my lapel, with the words of Isaiah 40:1-2 in Hebrew:

> Comfort ye, comfort ye my people, saith your God. Speak ye comfortably to Jerusalem, and cry unto her, that her warfare is accomplished, that her iniquity is pardoned: for she hath received of the Lord's hand double for all her sins.

"Now at last we have received the permission to establish our own state!" she cried. "And even Safed belongs to it, and Tiberias and all of the Galilee!"

Safed had from twelve thousand to thirteen thousand Arabs, and less than four thousand Jews. The Arabs were enraged because they would be under Jewish rule in the soon-to-be-established Jewish State. War broke out at once.

I had already bought all kinds of supplies in preparation for the arrival of my family, such as dried dates, grains, oil and whatever else was available. The truth is, when war starts, the supply of food stops.

I went to the Arab shopkeeper to buy olive oil. "You're not a Jew are you?" he asked me right away.

"No, I am not. You can see that in my face," I said.

"But maybe you're related to Jews?" he continued.

"I am not related to the Jews, but you are! You boast about being the children of Abraham and people like myself have come from far-away foreign countries to help you negotiate peace since you intend to fight with each other!"

I was able to buy oil and thus I had a satisfactory supply of food on hand. Soon my family would arrive. The food would be sufficient for some time, I thought. Come war or peace, I would remain in Safed and wait for my family.

The situation became more and more threatening. Then the Lord said to me, "You must leave this place."

"But why?" I asked in utter surprise. "I've come here on Your command and regardless of what may happen here, I trust that You are my help and my refuge. I am not going to leave now!"

But I was not at peace with myself about staying. It seemed like something was very wrong. Finally I said to the Lord, "I won't believe anything except for a clear command. Give me a passage from the Bible which speaks of this matter clearly so that I can make plans accordingly."

I prayed and opened the Bible at random. Rather startled, I stumbled upon the verse from Isaiah 26:20 that reads: "Come, my people, enter thou into thy chambers, and shut thy doors about thee: hide thyself as it were for a little moment, until the indignation be overpast."

This was my "clear command."

In the Midst of the Battle

As I was preparing to leave, a Jewish acquaintance advised me saying, "We never shoot at civilian buses. You will be able to travel safely on an Arab bus because you aren't a Jew."

So I took an Arab bus to Tiberias.

There I went to eat at a restaurant. The Arab owner was in a particular state of excitement. Noticing that I was not Jewish, he came to pour out his anger on me. "It's terrible that a Jewish nation is going to be established," he stormed. "Even Tiberias will be a part of it! Mark my words: We will kill all of the Jews in this city so that the Sea of Galilee will be red with their blood! Not one single Jew will ever live in this city!"

I was on my way to Jerusalem. At the bus station I saw that an Arab bus was about to leave for Jaffa so I decided to take it, in spite of the detour. When we arrived, a full-fledged war was in progress between Jaffa and its neighboring city of Tel Aviv.

(I heard later from some Christian nurses who understood Arabic, of the future plans of certain Arab leaders in Jaffa. The nurses happened to be walking behind two Arab leaders along a street in Tel Aviv, and overheard their conversation: "When we take control of Tel Aviv, I will take this commercial building here and you can take that one across the street. We'll kill the men and divide the women between us!")

When I arrived in Jaffa, the fighting was in full-force. Machine guns were crackling and fires were raging.

I was the only foreigner on the bus and when we reached our destination, an Arab came up to me and asked to see my passport. When he read "Suomi-Finland," he chuckled and said, "Fine! You are our friend! As you can see, we have some unrest here. Where are you headed?"

"I should get to Jerusalem," I replied.

"There won't be any buses leaving here tonight, but I know of a good hotel. I'll take you there."

He carried my suitcase and when we came to the hotel lobby, he introduced me as his "good friend, a Finnish gentleman," and told them to give me a decent room where I could sleep peacefully.

I was then led to a room and a moment later, my friend came to see what kind of room I had been given. The windows looked out onto the street.

"Why did they give you a room like this?" he wondered. "They could very well shoot right through the window. This will not do!" He went back to the office to reprimand the owners. "You can't give a Finn a room like that! A decent room means a safe one. Give him one at the back of the building so that he can sleep peacefully!"

The quiet room was at the end of an inside courtyard. After praying to the Lord for His continued direction on my trip, I went to sleep -in spite of the machine gun fire and the rumble of a distant battle.

Having had a good night's rest, I found an Arab bus downtown that was leaving for Jerusalem. We arrived safely and knowing it was the right thing to do, I went straight to the same American organization that had received me so warmly when I first arrived.

Miss Raedford was ill with fever. "It is good that you came!" she said. "I have been in rather bad shape. You can take care of tomorrow's meeting here at our place. I am not up to it now."

"Let's cancel it," I told her. "I can't conduct your meeting! I am not at all familiar with your manner of conducting a worship service!"

"No unnecessary formalities are needed!" was her response. "Preach the Word of God, that is all you need to do. Several younger brothers will be there and they will help you. The meeting must take place, especially since the Lord has sent a pastor precisely at the right moment!"

With great fear and trembling I agreed to lead the meeting.

I began the evening by explaining that Miss Raedford was ill and that I was a kind of substitute. Then I set the agenda, saying, "We will now read from God's Word, pray and sing." I also spoke about what the Lord had put on my heart.

At the end, someone came to tell me of a Finnish Christian named Elna Stenius who lived in Bethlehem. "Surely you would like to meet her?" he asked me.

"I certainly would," I answered. "In a foreign land, a citizen of one's home country is like a relative. Besides, what does it matter since as believers we are children of the same Father?" I took note of her address and decided to meet her the next day.

The rainy season was starting so I was in need of a decent hat. For this, I went into a Jewish shop and bought myself a hat that seemed to suit me well. Little did I know, this was a potentially fatal mistake. I had forgotten that the type of black felt hat I had just purchased always identifies Orthodox Jews. I was wearing the hat as I left for Bethlehem.

In Mortal Danger

The Arabs in Bethlehem are friendly people. Thus I had little trouble finding Elna Stenius. She welcomed me with joy. I explained to her how God had spoken to me and how He had called me to be among the Jewish people.

"Thank God," she said. "I've been here for over thirty years. Now the Lord is sending younger ones to the area. And I feel that my day-to-day work here is done. Soon it will end."

It was as if this veteran servant of God was passing a relay-race baton into my hands, to continue carrying the Gospel to His people. And in fact, only a few months after our meeting, Elna Stenius was taken home to be with the Lord.

Elna gave me much useful advice. For example, she told me of a truly significant event. In 1928 there had been a severe earthquake in Jerusalem. English geologists studied the Mount of Olives in the aftermath and reported to the city's government officials that earthquakes could be expected to occur at any time. The whole area is considered high-risk.

On the basis of that report, the English government in Jerusalem had refused all requests for building permits on the Mount of Olives. "It is likely that even the buildings now there will fall," was the response given to those requesting permits.

When I heard this, I was reminded of Zechariah's prophecy. He speaks of the Second Coming of the Messiah in chapter fourteen. He speaks of a time when the Jews will be persecuted. Nations that hate Jerusalem will assault her, looting and destroying.

And then the solution will come. Our Lord will act to save the remnant of His people, as written in Zechariah 14:4-5:

> And his feet shall stand in that day upon the mount of Olives, which is before Jerusalem on the east, and the mount of Olives shall cleave in the midst thereof toward the east and toward the west, and there shall be a very great valley; and half of the mountain shall remove toward the north, and half of it toward the south. And ye shall flee to the valley of the mountains; for the valley of the mountains shall reach unto Azal: yea, ye shall flee, like as ye fled from before the earthquake in the days of Uzziah king of Judah: and the Lord my God shall come, and all the saints with thee.

The 1928 geologists' report is in keeping with the Bible. The very earth is prepared, ready for the Lord's coming.

After Elna Stenius and I bade each other a warm farewell, I left to return to Jerusalem. It had begun to rain so I put on my hat and boarded an Arab bus.

On the way, there was a roadblock and every vehicle traveling to Jerusalem was stopped for inspection. The "inspectors" were Muslim extremists who had come to Bethlehem from Hebron. These are the kind who will occasionally shoot even at tourist buses.

I was the only foreigner on the bus. Two wild-looking Bedouins (Arab nomads) with daggers on their belts wriggled their way to me and began to speak to me excitedly in Arabic. I couldn't understand a single word they were saying. As I was not able to answer them, they dragged me out of the bus.

It's best to obey, I thought. *They could stick one of those daggers into my ribs.*

About twenty scary-looking men stood with machine guns on the side of the road. They pointed to the spot where they wanted me to stand in order to be shot.

At this time, enemy suspects were not examined very carefully. Not long before, a famous English archeologist who had been digging at a site near Hebron was murdered in a comparable situation. He had allowed his beard to grow and in general neglected his appearance. To avoid sunstroke, he wore a black hat. When the Arabs saw him, they automatically assumed that he was an Orthodox Jew and therefore shot him on the spot. Only after the fact did they inspect his papers and discovered that they had killed a well-known foreign archeologist.

Here I was, wearing on my head the same deadly mistake!

It seemed that I did not have much time left. Soon the guns would do the talking. I was surprised at myself for not being afraid at that moment. I folded my hands, closed my eyes and prayed, *Dear Heavenly Father! You called me to this land and I have obeyed You. Is this how short my life's work is to be? Dear Heavenly Father, You know that in Finland I have Maire and four children. I commit Maire and the children into Your care. If it is now my time to depart from this world then I will come to You by faith in the atoning power of Your Son's blood.*

Inside the bus, people began to take notice of what was going on outside. Suddenly a man rushed out and started to argue heatedly with the Arab gunman. I couldn't understand what they were saying, but I sensed that they were arguing about me. Then the man came to me and said in English, "I hope you have your passport with you."

When I replied that I did, he asked me to give it to him for a moment. He returned to the gunman. They examined it and looked at me to see whether I was the person pictured in the passport. Finally, they seemed to come to an agreement.

The stranger who had come to my rescue took me by the hand and led me back to the bus. The Arab commander ordered the roadblock to be removed and we continued on our journey. My helper sat down beside me and said, "You could now be lying on the side of the road. Do you know why I took the trouble to help you?"

I answered, "In all honesty, we've never met before, so I have no idea!"

"That's what you think," he retorted. "I was in the audience last night, at the BEM in Jerusalem where you led the meeting. I swore to the Arab commander that you were not Jewish but a Finnish Christian and that an innocent man should not be shot! I threatened him saying that if they did it, I would report the matter to the English military."

That one sermon in the Christmas of 1947 saved my life. But the hat that turned out to be such a dangerous article has remained unused. Never again have I put it on my head.

"We don't allow Jews on this side of the city," my helper said. "On which side did you want to get off?"

"I would like to return to the BEM," I replied.

"O.K., I'll come with you to help you get through. At present, a barbed-wire fence is being put up, and there is an opening in only one place." I was allowed to go through that opening, only because of my connection to my special helper!

It is possible that I was at this time the last outsider to visit Bethlehem, until 1967. That barbed wire fence was in place for twenty years, and only tourists with special permission were allowed to visit the town and its holy places. It was only in 1967 that the other side of Jerusalem, including Bethlehem, came under Israeli jurisdiction.

Saved Again

As I walked along the streets of Jerusalem, I met a man who asked me in wonderment, "Aren't you Syväntö, the one who was supposed to be in Safed? How come you're here now?"

Then he told me a story. "There's a terrible war going on up there. The Arabs intended to kill all of us Jews. I too left that city in a hurry. I was one of the city's merchants. You came to my shop from time to time."

He went on to describe the fate of my old home. "Both of the warring sides knew that the Scottish Mission was the strongest of all the houses in the city. The walls were one meter thick. We all assumed it to be the most secure place in town. But because both sides wanted it as their base, a terrible battle ensued. In the struggle, the entire house was blown up. And now nothing of it is left except for a pile of rubble."

Although everything I owned had been in the house that was destroyed, I thanked the Lord with my whole heart that He had led me out in time, with the verse from Isaiah.

I quickly wired my wife in Finland, advising her not to come. There was no place to come to. Our house had been destroyed.

When Maire received my telegram, she was with the children in Helsinki, awaiting passage on a Danish freighter. The children -Olavi (12), Kalervo (10), Rauha-Lilja (8) and Mirja (5)- were very disappointed when the long-awaited trip to Palestine had to be cancelled. They had already repeatedly told their friends that they were leaving for Palestine to eat oranges that were plentiful there! And now, father had sent them news like this!

The bad situation got worse. On the very day that the nation of Israel was established, the rioting started. The Arab terrorists killed as many Jews as they could, burned their homes and ransacked their businesses. A realistic description of these times is found in a book called *O Jerusalem*, a book truly worth reading.

Then even water in Jerusalem was rationed. It was pumped into the city from Rosh Ha Ain, seventy kilometers away, near the Lod airport. The Arabs had severed the pipeline. There was no water in the city except for that which fell as rain. Food supplies were all but finished. Jerusalem was in a state of siege. If an attempt was made to bring in something, the Arabs lying in ambush shot from both sides of the road at the supply vehicles. Many of these remain at the roadside to this day, as reminders of those perilous times. The situation in the city was truly critical.

Before Christmas I had paid a visit to Miss H.A. in Jerusalem. I had helped her with some menial tasks such as chopping firewood. Jerusalem is cold in the winter; sometimes it even snows. I urged her to go somewhere else, but she said, "I am not worried. All those around here are my good friends. I'm not going to leave." And she didn't. Not long afterwards, the Arabs shot her and her entire house was reduced to a pile of rubble.

How unfortunate that a dedicated Christian worker's life had to end in such a tragic way! It was certainly the grace of God and a miracle that amidst all this chaos I stayed alive and healthy.

Chapter 9

Back to Scandinavia

100-pound Stamps

In this period I was not able to do any work related to my calling. I had been away from Finland for a year and a half. I had made requests for currency transfers because Finnish money could not be used in Palestine, but the Bank of Finland always denied permission.

I wrote a letter to Sanfrid Mattson and told him about the Bethlehem incident where the Lord spared my life. I mentioned the destruction of my home in Safed and the chaotic situation in the country.

I also told him in my letter, that three times I had requested minimal sums to be transferred from the Bank of Finland -to no avail. I continued that I had thus far managed to get along in several foreign countries without my family, thanks to the Lord's mercy. Whereas the Bank of Finland had not been able to send me monies, God's bank had served its function according to the promise in the Bible, "Seek ye first the kingdom of God, and his righteousness; and all these things shall be added unto you" (Matthew 6:33). I ended the letter with the sentence, "To this day, the Lord has proved this to be true in my life" and I sealed the envelope with special postage stamps.

Sanfrid received the letter just as he was about to leave for America. In preparation, he went to the Bank of Finland on a business matter. As he was sitting in front of the bank manager, my letter accidentally fell from between the pages of his passport. An avid philatelist, he asked to see the stamps more closely and then exclaimed, "These are valuable Jerusalem postage stamps here! Do you have a friend there?"

"Yes, we do in fact," Sanfrid replied.

"What is the news from there now? I understand the country is in an awful state at present?" he queried.

"Well, yes. If you are interested, here is his letter. You may read it."

When I had written that letter, I didn't know that a manager of the Bank of Finland would be reading it. In it, I mentioned the fact that I had requested currency from the Bank three times, but each time in vain.

The man's expression changed after reading the letter, and then he said, "The financial situation has really been quite difficult but surely we could give him something." Then he said, "Christmas is at hand, I will write out a permit so that you can send him one hundred English pounds. Send it by telegram. Otherwise it won't arrive there because of the chaos."

Maire had in her possession enough marks from the sale of the farm so that she could pay for the telegram, and so the money "flew" to me in Jerusalem. I heard the explanation for this quick service only later when I arrived in Finland.

In the meantime, I had asked for a sign from God that if somehow He could get me money, I would know that I would be going home. Then the telegram arrived, announcing that one hundred English pounds had arrived for me!

"Smooth Sailing" with the Lord

I went to inquire about flights to Finland. At the travel agency I was informed that my best option was a KLM plane coming from Indonesia, on its way to Amsterdam. The ticket was 85 pounds.

"O.K.," I told the ticket agent, "but the trip from Jerusalem to Lod is dangerous to travel. The Arabs are often in ambush along the sides of the road. I will buy a ticket on condition that you will arrange a trip along a safe route to the airport."

My proposition was discussed for a while, followed by a suggestion: For an extra five pounds I would be taken to the airport. I would need to spend the night in a designated hotel from which a driver would come to pick me up early in the morning. He was to knock on my door in a special code. "You are to follow him without asking any questions. He will take you there safely," they assured me.

"That's fine," I said and paid the ninety pounds.

On the day before departure, I had to arrange for a permit to leave the country as well as a re-entry permit so that I wouldn't lose my valuable visa.

At the passport office, I was confronted by a terrible sight. Somewhere nearby a bomb had exploded. The windows were smashed and birds were flying about in the room. Passports were strewn here, there and everywhere. Somewhere among them was my to-be-stamped passport!

Fortunately, I found it in a corner. When one of the employees walked by, I explained to him my situation. He promised to have my documents ready for the next day, as the person authorized to sign my papers was not in at that moment. I of course had no choice but to accept this answer, so I left the office praying that my request would indeed be taken care of.

I was not disappointed. The following day it was ready! I stationed myself in the hotel to wait for my ride.

Between two and three in the morning, I heard the appropriate knocks on my door. A wild-looking Arab motioned me to follow him to a small passenger car waiting outside. I noticed its many bullet holes and thought to myself, *this will not be the first dangerous trip taken with this automobile*! The man pushed me into the back seat, told me to lie down and said, "Whatever happens, you must remain absolutely silent!"

To this day, I don't know what roads we took to Lod but we got there. The trip lasted at least two hours. It seems that he drove by way of Samaria.

My trip to the Bromma airport in Stockholm was long and tedious. First there was a six-hour flight on a KLM propeller plane to Rome (which today seems ridiculous). Then we continued on to Amsterdam where I stayed overnight. I arrived in Sweden late the next day.

I was tired as I called Alvar Lindskog, the director of *Ostermalms Fria Forsamling*, to ask whether I could stay the night at his house.

He was ecstatic. "Thank God you have arrived from Palestine alive! Of course you can come! The airport bus passes our place. We are waiting to hear your news."

Kaarlo Syväntö

I went to buy a ticket to the city. In my pocket I had the remaining Palestinian pounds which I had received in Jerusalem. These were refused. I was told, "This money is worthless, the State of Palestine is in chaos."

"I need to get to Stockholm for the night," I explained. "I don't have any other kind of money."

Behind me someone overheard the conversation.

"Maybe I can help you," he suggested. "Here are fifty crowns. You can get started with this."

"Thank you!" I exclaimed. "Please give me your name and address so that I can repay you," I said.

The next day I returned the loan in the mail.

Thus I arrived in Stockholm! It was already about midnight. A handful of friends were waiting for me, with refreshments including strong coffee! We spoke until 2:00 A.M. and then I began to yawn with increasing frequency. Finally my host whispered in my ear, "We plan to send you off to sleep at a Finnish doctor's house. We don't know Finnish and he knows very little Swedish. The man is at a crossroads in his life and perhaps you can help him to find what he is looking for!"

And so the next two hours were spent speaking with the young Finnish doctor who was indeed ready to accept salvation in Christ. Rejoicing, I laid my head on the pillow at about 4:00 A.M.!

The plane was to leave for Finland at eight o'clock the next morning. At seven, Lindskog came to pull me out of bed. "Do you know where you are?" he asked. I must have looked lost as he tried to wake me up.

I mumbled, "Yes.... We're in the airplane, aren't we? A while ago we left Marseilles and I suppose we'll soon be in Amsterdam...."

"What? You are not on a plane. You are in Stockholm! Here's some black coffee. Drink it fast so that you can clear your mind and get to the plane for Finland on time!"

While I was drinking the coffee he asked me about my family. "How many children do you have and how old are they?"

"Two boys and two girls," I answered. I even remembered their birthdays. Before we left, Lindskog made a quick phone call.

The taxi was waiting for us. We took off at full speed but on the way, Lindskog asked the driver to stop for a minute. He went somewhere and came back with a huge package. "Here are some wool sweaters as gifts for your children," he said, handing me the bundle.

The airline employee looked at my things questioningly and said, "Your baggage is limited to the regular weight and besides, what is this package?"

Pointing to Lindskog, I explained that he had given me Christmas gifts to take to my children.

"It will cost you extra to bring it because it is over the allowed weight," she insisted.

My friend reacted quite strongly. "What is this? This traveler has already survived robbers and murderers and arrived here safe and sound. It is a downright shame to require payment from him! Let him go!"

The person weighing the luggage thought for a moment and then waved me on saying, "Fine, you can go!"

The Family Adrift

When I arrived in Helsinki, it was freezing cold, 25 degrees below Celsius. In Palestine it had been +25 degrees! I was not dressed warmly enough and there was a long line of people waiting for a taxi.

Shivering from cold, I went to the airport bus driver and said, "This is really strange! I've survived many bad situations, from robbers to dangers in a war zone but this snow storm and freezing weather are what seem to be stopping me in my tracks!"

"Take your things and go behind that corner," he suddenly said, pointing. "I'll take you!"

This kind driver made a special trip just for me. I went to the home of Lauri Pietilä, one of the veteran friends of Israel in Finland.

In the morning, I began the search for my family. First I called Odin Finell, the overseas Christian workers' secretary of our congregation at the time. When he heard my voice, he literally shouted, "Thank God that you have come home alive!"

"There have indeed been many dangers and adventures but do you know where Maire and the children are?" I asked.

"Your telegram arrived just in time, preventing their departure. They are all well, living near Salo."

Maire had been at her wit's end for a long time, since she had received my telegram. She had sold our home at Ilmajoki to evangelist August

Vartiainen, so she no longer had a home. There was no going back nor was it possible to move on. Maire had sighed, *Dear Heavenly Father, show us what we are to do now and where we are to go, since even our things have already passed through customs!*

Unexpectedly, she met a schoolmate and teaching colleague at the Stockmann's department store Christmas sale. "Maire!" she had exclaimed. "You are supposed to be in Palestine!"

"Yes that's right, but Kaarlo wired that I should not come. A war is going on there."

To this the colleague answered, "Listen. My mother is ill and staying at Nousiainen. I will be with her over the holidays. Here are the keys to the school at Salo. Go there. You will find plenty of food supplies. Make yourselves at home!"

So I found my family at the Salo School,. It was a happy reunion for all of us!

At the Teemassaari School

Of course we couldn't stay there forever, as a new semester was about to begin. Together we placed our hope in our Heavenly Father, asking Him what to do next.

Then Maire noticed an advertisement in a teacher's journal, for a teaching position at the Teemassaari School on Rantasalmi, an island off Finland's west coast. The job was open as of January 1. It was a miracle! The school's head teacher had decided to retire at the beginning of the new year instead of at the end of the school year. The timing for her retirement was an exception to the rule.

It was not long before Maire received a positive reply to her application.

Upon arrival at Varkaus, we went to visit a Christian businessman named Koivisto. When he saw us, he said, "You are really lucky! The old teacher has just left and the men from the village who brought her things from the island can make the return trip with you. They have a horse and sleigh, otherwise it would be difficult to cross over on the ice to get there."

At that time there was no other mode of transportation to the island, so we wrapped the children in blankets and into the sleigh we went. That trip was particularly hard for Rauha-Lilja. Although she didn't complain on the journey, she told us later that she had never been so cold in her life... It was -20 degrees Celsius and a cold wind was blowing.

A dismal sight awaited us at the school. We found only empty, cold rooms. The teacher had obviously taken all her possessions with her. So we asked the men if we could borrow the blankets for a start. By dawn we had all "thawed out," having made a blazing fire in the fireplace.

Each morning God's mercy is new and His faithfulness great. The next day we began to collect the bits and pieces that are needed in every home. And so our life continued.

The Summer of 1948 in Norway

As I mentioned earlier, at the time, the importance of work among Jews was not at all understood, neither in Finland nor in Sweden. In Norway, however, the situation was different. I had befriended the secretary of the Pentecostal Church in Norway, Gunnerius Tollefsen, a former Christian worker in Africa. In addition to his other duties on the field, he had translated the New Testament into an African language and had been granted a Ph.D. for that reason. He was a generous, noble character, and a warm-hearted Christian. He was also the foster-father of Emanuel Minos, a well-known preacher in Scandinavia.

Tollefsen had heard of my arrival in Finland and wrote me a kind letter which read something like this:

> Dear Kaarlo, please pay us a visit. We will try to help you. I will give you a good recommendation and with that as an opening you will be able to make the rounds of the various congregations in this country.

When I received his letter I had only just recovered from a sciatic-nerve problem. To come from temperatures of +25 degrees to the cold of Finland was cause enough for this illness. My home cure was sauna baths, and finally the pain subsided. So a month into my stay in Finland I was already off to Norway.

Norway gave me a very warm welcome. In Oslo I was able to participate in the first course ever for workers among Jews. My fellow students all shared the same calling to Palestine, one from Sweden and the rest from Norway. Our teacher was a former rabbi. This was his calling, to teach the group of about ten students in this special intensive course.

I spent that summer of 1948 in Norway. Together with a Swedish brother, we made trips from Oslo to Tromssa and even to the Lofoott Islands. My traveling and preaching companion was very slow-paced, a fact which caused me much distress. It seems to have been part of God's patience training for me, as I tend to be rather impatient by nature. Even at mealtimes I was put to the test; my partner spent at least an hour eating while I finished in a matter of minutes. I compensated for the waste of time (in my opinion!) by bringing my Bible with me to the dining room.

On one occasion when we planned to leave Tromssa to go south, we bought tickets the night before. That evening we were at a service until quite late and so we got to sleep only at a late hour. Very early the next morning my companion woke me up, saying, "Get up fast, you need to pack! We are leaving soon!" I looked at my watch and it was 4:00 A.M.. We had gone to bed at 11:30 P.M. I told him, "What is the point of rushing around so early? The bus doesn't leave until 8:00 A.M.! Let me sleep in peace!" I woke up at 7:30 A.M., packed my suitcase and even helped my buddy who was still busy packing his things. Then when we boarded the bus, he stroked the stubble on his chin and complained, "For goodness' sake, I've been in such a hurry that I didn't even have time to shave!"

Preparing for the Return Trip

In the fall of 1948, my return visa to Israel was due to expire, so I began to plan my return trip. In my absence, Israel had officially become a nation, on May 15, 1948. But I was in danger of losing my permanent visa.

All of our possessions were still at customs in Helsinki. I requested that they be sent to Oslo so that I could take them with me on the freighter to Israel. A couple of days prior to departure, the travel agency notified me that they required 1,110 crowns for transporting the baggage. *Since I already have my ticket,* I thought to myself, *surely I shouldn't have to pay such an exorbitant sum for baggage.*

"With your ticket you are allowed to take one cubic meter of baggage. You have six cubic meters of furniture and other things. Besides, you are responsible for the transportation and harbor costs accrued in their transport from Helsinki to Oslo. This bill has to be paid before you leave."

I did not have money for such a bill. It had taken great effort just to find enough money for my ticket to travel. So I prayed, *Dear Heavenly Father, You know that these are all our possessions, which I should get to Israel. Where in the world can I now get the required money? Please take care of this matter since I cannot. I don't intend to speak to anyone about this situation. If You don't arrange it, then these things will simply stay here.*

I noticed in the newspaper that a certain pastor I knew from my summer travels in northern Norway was in Oslo holding meetings. His sermon was to be on the topic "fulfillment of prophecies." He was a friendly man and I so I called him to say that I would be going back to Israel in a few days. I bid him farewell and expressed my thanks to him for all the kindness he had shown me during the past summer. Suddenly he said, "Hey! We are not parting like this, are we? Come to the service this evening and we'll have a visit afterwards."

So I went, and shortly before the close of the service, the brother announced to the audience, "Among us tonight is Kaarlo Syväntö, a man with a calling to Israel. He is leaving the day after tomorrow." Then addressing me directly, he said, "If you are here, please come and share with us that which is on your heart. We have just spoken about the incredible fulfillment of prophecies that is happening in our day. The nation of Israel has been established, and you have been there to witness it! Come, this audience will be glad to hear from you."

I rose up in my seat and told them about my calling and about some of my experiences in Palestine. I also mentioned that I would indeed be starting on my trip in a couple of days and that I would be grateful for their prayers on my behalf. But I didn't mention a single word about my baggage and my need for money.

When I finished, the pastor turned again to the congregation and said, "A while ago we had a sacrificial offering to cover the costs of this meeting place. Now we have a special opportunity to do something for the work in Israel. Why don't we take another offering and give it to this brother to cover his travel costs?"

A murmur of approval was heard from all over the room, and the collection baskets were sent around. When the meeting ended we went to talk and pray for a while in a back room. The ushers came in, emptied the baskets into a bag and said, "We won't bother to count this, here you have a gift from God for your trip!"

In the hotel, I poured the contents of the bag on the bed and sorted the money in separate piles. It was enough to cover the cost of transporting my baggage!

At the Very Last Moment

I had a final obstacle to overcome before leaving Norway. The enemy of our souls still tried to block me. At the shipping office I was asked, "How old are you? We forgot to ask you earlier."

"I was born in 1909," I answered.

The employee continued, "An order has been received from the United Nations that travelers under forty years of age bound for Israel cannot travel. It is feared that they will join the warring factions, either on the Arab or the Jewish side, and thus prolong the conflict."

"What should I do?" I asked.

"You will have to get an entry permit to Jerusalem from the Peace Commission of the United Nations."

I got the Commission's address and sent a quick telegram, asking them to reply by wire to the Swedish Orient Lines office who had to receive confirmation that the matter had been cleared. I no longer remember where the money for the telegram came from. I prayed earnestly that the reply would arrive in time.

One hour before the ship's departure, I called from Oslo to the Gothenburg ship office to ask whether they had had word from the United Nations.

"No," was the reply. "We're sorry, but we cannot let you come aboard the ship. Under no circumstances will we violate the orders of the United Nations."

At that moment the Lord told me, "Don't be in a hurry! Talk to this man a little longer."

"But isn't there still one whole hour before the ship is due to leave?" I tried telling him.

"Well, yes, but time is running out. If a reply has not arrived yet, it will not get here on time. It's wisest to take the next ship."

I kept on insisting. "But all our baggage is already on this ship!"

"We have enough time to throw it ashore within the hour!"

Although my tone of voice was calm, I was actually quite distressed. *Would I really be left off this ship?*

Just as I was about to end the conversation, he shouted: "Just a minute! An errand boy is coming with some kind of paper in his hand."

I could hear the rustle of paper over the phone, as the letter was being opened. It was my reply: *Permission granted*!

"Thank you very much!" I told him. But after I put down the receiver, my faithful Lord and Savior heard more than one "thank you" from me!

Chapter 10

Back in the Promised Land

My New Friend the Rabbi

As I boarded the ship, the captain told me that in addition to myself, there were no other passengers on board except the chief rabbi of Sweden and his family. I wondered how the Lord had managed to lead me into such refined company! I sat at the same table with the captain and the rabbi.

An elderly man, the rabbi turned out to be very friendly and easy-going. His daughter even took the trouble to teach me Hebrew during the five weeks of our journey. We were together a great deal, stopping at many of the ports on the way.

Both the rabbi and I liked to rise early and to go out on deck. One morning as we were nearing our destination, there was a beautiful sunrise. The Mediterranean was very calm as I walked along the deck admiring the breath-taking scene.

I noticed the rabbi sitting at his usual place. When he saw me, he motioned for me to sit in the chair next to him. I was surprised to see that he was reading the New Testament! He had an English Bible, open to the second chapter of Acts where we find the story of Pentecost in Jerusalem.

Back in the Promised Land

He set the book aside and began to question me. Did I have a family? Was I going to Israel for the first time? Did I plan to stay long? Was I going there as a tourist? And what was my occupation?

I sighed to the Lord for His help, asking Him whether or not I should tell the rabbi my story just as it was. The Lord replied that I could, without fear.

So I explained, "I am not a pastor or a theologian. I am a former railroad employee. During the war, in a risky situation, I promised the Lord that if He would save me, He could use me in whatever corner of the world He wished. He performed a miracle and helped me - and later gave me a calling to be among your people. My purpose is to give God's Word to your nation. First, Hebrew Bibles which are needed in schools, and then to new immigrants in their own language. We will always give Bibles which include the New Testament."

"We do not have any kind of support network," I continued. "We are just an ordinary single family with no promise of assistance from anywhere. We believe that the Lord will help us in this valuable endeavor. God has confirmed his calling to me in many ways, including providing my family with an immigration permit to Israel, from the English government."

"We rejoice in the fact that God is gathering His own people back to the land of their fathers, and we believe that He blesses and helps you. We pray on behalf of your country and its people. Personally, I consider it a great privilege that I can, in a small way, share in the rebuilding of your nation and be with your people."

He listened without saying a word while I spoke. When I finished he said, "Thank you for trusting me, so that you related all this to me so openly. We need all kinds of rebuilding. We need it in the *kibbutzes*, in factories, on farms, in construction work, but our greatest need is in the spiritual rebuilding of our people. The best thing that you can do is give us Bibles, God's Word, and especially those that include the New Testament."

After a moment, he continued. "Should you have any kind of problems with the government in regard to your work, you may with complete trust turn to me. I will help you whenever I can. Don't be afraid at all if you find yourself in difficulties. Turn to me. I promise to help you."

Then he took a business card from his pocket and handed it to me. It read: "Professor H.B., University Dean." He had served as Presiding Chief Rabbi in Sweden when the former one had passed away. A new one had now been appointed so he was returning to his regular position as dean of the Hebrew University of Jerusalem. At his home, a secret group of "Nicodemus Christians" gathered for Bible study on each Sabbath from four to six o'clock. I have had the opportunity to be present with them a few times. There are some high Israeli government officials among them.

It was this kind of valuable friendship that I was able to make on the trip to Israel. No wonder the devil tried in every way to prevent me from making the journey on this particular ship!

This same dean invited me to the twenty-fifth anniversary of the university. Those were difficult days, since the original campus was left on the Arab side, on the foothills of Mount Scopus. The celebration was held at a Catholic high school building since a new university building had not yet been constructed.

The "cream" of the entire Jewish world came to this important event. I was amazed to find myself among them, to have been remembered by the dean and to have been shown this kind of respect.

It so happened that Lewi Pethrus was visiting my home in Tiberias at the time. We discussed all kinds of things and it seemed that this honorable servant of the Lord was rather doubtful on many issues. He happened to notice on my desk, the invitation from the Hebrew University. He read it and exclaimed, "I should also attend such a celebration. How may I get an invitation?"

"I don't know where you could get one," I replied. "I have the impression that such invitations are given as personal favors."

After the ceremony, a wonderful dinner was held at the large YMCA auditorium, to which only those with invitations were admitted. As I sat among this prestigious group, I folded my hands under the table and prayed, *Dear Heavenly Father! May these, the finest of the Jewish people, experience the fulfillment of Your promise, and the outpouring of Your Spirit upon them so that miracles would happen in their midst! Let that time come soon*!

Pioneering in Tel Aviv

I decided to look for a certain Messianic family who had lived on the Jaffa side of Tel Aviv. I was afraid of what may have happened to them because the War of Independence had been fought particularly in their area.

Then I heard from someone that they had been able to escape shortly before the uprising began. They had a small plot of land, about one hectare in size, at Herzliyya, on the outskirts of Tel Aviv. There was no house on the property. It had been dismantled. But the family lived in what they had managed to find: an old railroad car, without wheels and much smaller than the ones I was accustomed to in Finland (railroad tracks are narrower in Israel). In this car the entire family resided, including six children, a grandmother and the parents.

There was also a small tool shed on the property. When I found the family, I told them I would gladly help them in any way I could.

"Of course we need help," they answered. "We need to begin building a home and to clear away the garbage. But where can we house you?"

"Well, you have that old tool shed over there," I said. It was perhaps two meters in length and one and a half meter wide, with a corrugated steel roof. Made of sparsely nailed wooden planks, the wind blew through the cracks. After the axes, hoes and shovels were removed, a bed could be fitted against the wall. This then was my home for the next six months. A Finnish pigpen would honestly have been a better "hole;" it would have been warmer! The nights in Israel can be quite cold and damp, particularly during the rainy season.

I began my job of clearing away the debris, only to find that the place was teeming with snakes! Thus my first job in this country was that of a snake killer! Once when I was lifting a rather heavy gatepost, Mr. O--- shouted from behind me, "Drop that! There's a horrid creature in the bottom of the pit. Your hands were very close to it." It turned out to be a two-meter long viper. After we killed it, we put the carcass under a sack and went to eat. "Let's leave it there," I said. "When our guests from Tel Aviv arrive this evening, we'll let them take a look at the kind of creatures that roam around here."

While we were eating, the children shouted from the yard, "Dad, dad! Come quickly! Our *Mirri* (pet cat) has found a horrible snake under a sack and she's dragging it underneath the house!"

The family cat had indeed caught scent of the "goodies" and decided to take his meal in peace, under the shed. We arrived too late. Mirri's feast was in full swing and she took no heed of the children's appeals to come out of her hiding place.

"How awful," they complained. "If our Mirri eats a poisonous snake won't she die from the poison?"

A crunching sound was heard as the cat dined. When she had had her fill, she barely squeezed out of the crevice into which she had so lithely entered, minus a full stomach! But nothing happened, the cat survived without so much as a stomachache!

Everything was still rationed, as it was in Finland. I was able to eat as long as I worked for the family. However, one day my meal had a somewhat "unpleasant price tag." The father of the family asked me whether I had ever killed anything other than snakes.

"No, I guess not," I answered. "Of course in theory I know how animals are butchered in Finland. First they knock the animal unconscious and then an artery is opened to allow the blood to drain."

"Our goat had two kids," he said. "One of them a billy goat. That wretched thing is eating all of our green vegetables and even the seedlings of our fruit trees! If I hire a licensed butcher, the affair would be handled as a public matter and then we wouldn't have anything left for ourselves. It would be nice to eat our own billy goat. If you could end its life you would be doing us all a great service."

I was hesitant at first, but I remembered that I had promised the Lord to do everything that helps His "business." Perhaps this too was in some way related to that promise. I took the billy goat into my arms and carried him to a distance. After the job was done, I prepared the meat into appropriate cuts and took them to a very grateful father of the family.

As the butcher, I received a generous helping of delicious steak, and who was I to refuse that which I had earned!

Picking Oranges

Our neighbor had a large grove of orange trees. In the fall of 1948, the war was still going on even against Egypt, and all able-bodied men were at the front lines. For the harvest, young children from eight to ten years of age were recruited as pickers.

One day their supervisor, an elderly man, came to me and said, "We desperately need an adult to help in getting the crates of oranges into the warehouse. The children aren't strong enough to do it, and I am not well. Couldn't you come to work for a while at the orchard? Maybe your employer would lend you to me."

"I suppose so," my boss replied. "We'll try to get along without you. Go help the old man!"

The neighbor had promised to pay me fairly good wages and so I changed employers. I continued however, to live in the tool shed. Winter came and with it the winter rains. It was cold at night, and I was hungry. Of course I had as many oranges as I wanted but one needs something more than fruit for sustenance.

Payday was postponed again and again. My diary from that period is solemn: "Money all gone. Bread all gone. Dreadfully hungry. No food...." For two months I didn't receive a single penny. The owner was away in America, to which communication was difficult, and I was too ashamed to go to my former employer and suggest we butcher the other goat... They had their own troubles in providing for a nine-member family.

In this school of patience I lost over ten kilos. Perhaps it was good for me! It was a genuine "orange fast." The old grandmother was the only one who appeared to be led by the Lord. One day, when I was suffering from extreme hunger pangs, she came and knocked on the tool-shed door. When I opened it, she thrust a half-loaf of bread into my hands. She was to me like Elijah's raven! That bread was rationed out to last many days.

Finally, after two months, the day of reckoning arrived. I received my money and bubbling with joy, I immediately made my way to the store three and a half kilometers away.

In my hut I had no light so when evening fell it was pitch black. I couldn't read my Bible so I devoted myself to prayer.

So as I was buying food I also asked for some kerosene and a small lamp. "It is rationed," the storekeeper said.

"I am at work every day from morning until night. I simply don't have the time to stand in line with a ration card. Couldn't you give me just a little bit of oil so that I could read at night? Otherwise the time passes so slowly."

"Find yourself a kerosene can from somewhere and I'll give you a liter or so," the storekeeper replied. He gave me three liters of lamp oil. It was like a gift from heaven, for now I was able to read the Bible in the evenings.

The harvesting of oranges continued. Once there was a powerful storm that caused a large number of oranges to fall from the trees. It rained heavily for three days. I didn't want to take leave from work without a good reason, so I put on my "Made in Finland"-raincoat and rubber boots. Without hesitation, I went out and picked the fallen fruit into crates and carried them into the warehouse. If oranges remain for long on the ground, especially in mud, they are no longer suitable for export.

When the storm finally subsided, the supervisor came to me, bewailing the loss. "How terrible! All this damage to our oranges since they have been on the ground for three days already!"

"There has been no damage." I said. "Let's go and see."

Under the trees there were only a few oranges here and there but the warehouse was stocked with a fair number of full crates.

The man stared at me with eyes wide open for a while, silent. Then he said, "I've never seen this kind of a miracle. How in the world were you able to pick the fruit during such a storm?"

"Well, there was plenty of room here to work while it was raining," I said. "And besides, why should an able-bodied man needlessly take days off from work?"

"When we establish a kibbutz we will invite you to become the first honorary founding member! This country needs men of your kind," my employer said, complimenting me.

My job at the grove also included the task of carrying the crates to the warehouse on a donkey. For that purpose, one had to learn the Hebrew commands since the donkey had learned to understand that language! In the evening I let the donkey out to roam. In the mornings I had quite a task before I succeeded in catching the animal in order to harness him for work; he liked grazing and sleeping more than carrying crates of oranges. The morning "ceremonies" always involved a chase with shouts of *dio* (the Hebrew command to work for a donkey), which sounds like "dear" in English. And so I would run around shouting, "Dear, dear, to work, to work!"

Once the fruit was harvested, the soil around the trees had to be fertilized. When this was done, my job at the orange grove was also finished.

Carrots, Carrots and more Carrots!

My former employer and his family were happy to have me back with them. They had planted a large area with carrots. So my next job was to thin out the field of carrots.

I started work early in the morning and continued until late in the evening. The sun shone like a flaming fireball. My head and my back ached as I thinned out the green garden. The only thing in my mind was carrots, carrots and more carrots!

The devil came to me and sneered, *Now look. This is what it has come to. Working for God pulling carrots! This experience won't even be of any use to you in the future!*

I would answer, "Be quiet, you liar! My Lord knows when this phase of my life will end."

One evening I had a splitting headache. My employer's wife came to my shack to scold me. "Listen. The job has been done rather carelessly. In some places the carrots are still crowded and in others they are too sparse."

"It may be so," I replied. "All day I've had such a severe headache that it has hindered my vision."

After she left, I turned with a sigh to the Lord, *Oh Heavenly Father! Will you ever decide to stop this phase? I'm beginning to resent seeing nothing but carrots...!*

A Different Kind of Job Proposition

The Lord heard my prayer. The next day I received a letter from the Scottish Mission in Tiberias. The head doctor wrote: "The Mission hospital has been a hospital for soldiers. Now it has been given back to us. We need a trustworthy person who could be in full charge of the hospital when I leave for my home country. The hospital should be put into good condition for our own use. You have been recommended for this task. Can you come?"

I replied by letter that I would. When the family I worked for heard this, they were shocked. "You, a 'northerner' will never survive in Tiberias! It is so hot there that no one like you has even tried to live there as long as they have had a choice. You won't survive there for long. It is impossible! Cancel your promise right away! You don't know what you have done."

Thus I wrote another letter and stated that I heard Tiberias is so hot and unhealthy a place that "northerners" can't live there.

When I had sent the letter, the Lord asked me, "With whose permission did you send that letter of cancellation? Tiberias is precisely the place where I want you to live."

I became frightened and said, *Dear Lord, forgive me! Truly I did not think of asking You about it. But should the doctor still ask me to come, it will be a sign that I must go.*

The doctor didn't believe me. He sent a telegram saying to come to the Lod airport at such and such a time. When I arrived, he was about to get on a flight for Scotland. He shoved a bunch of keys into my hand and said, "Here are the keys, take care of the hospital until I return!"

That was the extent of our conversation. He had to rush to board the plane.

Chapter 11

In Tiberias

The Scottish Mission

The Scottish Mission of Tiberias has faithfully served the people of this country. In the beginning of the last century, there was a great revival in Scotland, and one of its results was that a Christian doctor named David Torrence was sent to Israel. Truly a man of God, he came during the period of Turkish rule. The Muslims, of course, would not have wanted to receive Christians in this country, but because health conditions were so critical, they readily accepted a Christian doctor! Malaria, cholera, typhoid fever, and many other diseases were rampant.

The Lord blessed Dr. Torrence' activities and he was able to establish the Scottish Mission Hospital in 1894. The work was a great blessing and of benefit to many. Having completed his "day's work," he died and was buried in the adjoining cemetery on the shore of the Sea of Galilee.

His son, contrary to his father, was a real "tightwad" who loved money. This was Dr. Herbert Torrence, who had so carelessly hired me at the airport and authorized me to be a kind of supervisor of the hospital during his absence.

During the latter part of May 1949, I arrived in Tiberias, only to discover just how critically the Mission was in need of a supervisor.

I saw this as soon as I opened the church door. It had obviously not been used for years as a house consecrated to the Lord. The reed organ had been broken to pieces and all kind of filth, including human excrement was strewn all over the floor. The building had been used as a latrine, and an indescribable stench assaulted anyone coming in the room.

I flung the door wide open, opened the windows and found a shovel and a broom. After a few hours the work was done and I was satisfied with the results.

Fortunately, the other buildings were not in such bad shape but there was still plenty of repairing to be done. The rats were a nuisance on the entire site and in the decaying buildings. I waged a war against them by setting traps and snares. In fact, I fought them day and night, with sticks or whatever else was longer than my arm. At first I had doubts as to who would win the battle, but finally the two-footed creature conquered the four-footed ones. I even kept a record of how many vermin I killed on a daily basis.

The orchard suffered from drought. The trees and shrubs were drooping in the heat so I began to water them. Gradually the green returned, and beautiful flowers came forth.

The head doctor from the Nazareth EMMS Hospital came now and then to observe my activities and to pay my wages. I received one English pound per day, and since I lived alone, I could live on that.

Looking for a Home

The time had come to have my family arrive in the country. Maire and the children had moved to Sweden and lived near Boras where Maire had found work at a factory, sewing.

"We would be glad to be able to be with you," my wife answered. "Can't you find any place for us to rent?"

I went to Jerusalem to make inquiries. An American organization had its own place in the center of the city. An English pastor had rented the entire complex. I went to visit him and explained that my family in Sweden was anxiously waiting to travel to Israel.

"I have taken over this big house," he said. And big it was, including a church and a three-story building with many rooms. "We are brothers, are we not?" he continued. "Choose the best rooms in the building, pay a little for the water and electricity and bring your family here!"

"Thank you for your kind offer! I will consider it until tomorrow morning. I've just arrived from a trip, and I am rather tired. By morning I'll have new energy."

I went to my room, knelt beside the bed and prayed, *Dear Heavenly Father! By morning I need to make an important decision. Should I bring my family here to Jerusalem or what should I do? I don't dare make any decision unless You, Lord, give me a clear answer and either show me that my place is here or somewhere else.*

Having prayed, I went to sleep. The Lord showed me a remarkable dream. In that dream, morning had come, and I went to see the Englishman. We walked on the third floor. There was a splendid suite with a view of the entire city. It was very accommodating, with two rooms and a kitchen - as if it were made for us. Even the cost was more than reasonable. We agreed that I would take it. But after our agreement, I went once again to view the house. In the corner of a certain room, I noticed a curtain, and drawing it aside, I observed a strange iron door on the upper part of which there was a huge beam with an old-fashioned padlock hanging on it. I pondered for a long time what this thick beam could possibly safeguard.

"It seems that everything here is in order," I said to the pastor. "But what secret is hidden behind that door?"

"I have my personal collection there. As you know our lives as ministers are often quite monotonous, so we need some kind of hobby. During my free time, I tame wild animals. Due to other people, I must keep them hidden. If they were to know, a great fuss would be raised! But this will in no way bother you."

"What mysterious wild animals?" I wondered.

"This is a private matter, don't bother with unnecessary questions," the pastor replied. "Everything is under control and you need not worry about it."

But I needed to know what kind of wild animals lived behind the door. Then I noticed that the lock was not properly closed. I jerked it off and pulled the iron door open.

Never in my life had such a horrible sight confronted me. The devil himself sat in a corner of the dark room. Two giant snakes were on each side like bodyguards. Eyes green, glowing in anger, the creature stared at me and the snakes hissed at me.

The devil looked very angry. I even noticed horns on his head, as he is usually portrayed in pictures.

I slammed the door shut and said, "When those dreadful creatures get loose, they will destroy your life and this entire place. Never will I come to live in this house, you can be sure of that!"

I woke from the dream in the middle of the night. I had received a clear answer that I had asked for in the evening.

The pastor was unusually friendly the next morning. "How did you sleep?" he asked.

"Very well, thank you!"

"Shall we go look at the rooms?" he asked.

"No, we won't. This house is not the place for me. The Lord showed me that clearly last night." I didn't explain further nor did he question me about it.

A House on the Lakeshore

So I began to pray again, *Dear Father in Heaven, Maire keeps pestering me about a home. Please provide us with a dwelling place!*

I returned to search in Tiberias and found Dr. Heart's house. Dr. Heart, the founder of the YMCA, had upon retirement, bought a small piece of land from some Russian nuns and built himself a beautiful winter home. There he had maintained a valuable collection of fine art. The house was set in a grove of trees, along the shore of the Sea of Galilee. In earlier times the house had been in good condition and likely a very nice place to live.

Dr. Heart was a Messianic believer who had helped to free POWs during WWI. He had served for a time as a guide and interpreter for a wealthy American in Jerusalem. Once, he commented about his desire to establish a YMCA in Jerusalem but due to a lack of funds this was impossible. He even mentioned that he knew of a place in the center of the city, available at a low price.

In Tiberias

When the wealthy American was leaving the country, he handed a check to Dr. Heart and said, "Here is some money. It will be enough to buy something, won't it?"

The check was for one million dollars. This occurred in 1925.

Dr. Heart bought the land he had mentioned and established the Jerusalem YMCA. A magnificent hotel with three hundred rooms now stands on the property, adorned by a tower fifty-two meters high.

On one side of the entrance is Dr. Heart's name, and on the other side, the name of the donor, J.N. Jarvie. Professor Saarisalo and many other knowledgeable people have said that Jarvie was originally *Järvi*, a Finnish name.

Dr. Heart died shortly before WWII. Upon request from the YMCA, no one was assigned to live at his Tiberias home. Whoever had been there since had stolen the art, books, and any furniture it had contained. The last residents had even taken the doors and windows with them.

So it was this deserted, windowless and doorless stone house, three kilometers from Tiberias, that I happened to come upon in my search for a home. *This would be a really fine place to live,* were my first thoughts. *If only it could be put into good condition*! I decided to visit the YMCA office in Jerusalem.

"I found your deserted house in Tiberias. Would you rent it to me as I am planning to invite my family to join me in this country?" I asked.

The director responded, "How can anyone possibly live there, since it doesn't even have doors or windows!"

"What if I should get them from Finland? If I may live there for three years rent-free, I will get doors and windows for it," I promised.

So it was agreed and a contract made to that effect.

Then I sent word to Maire that they could come! A house had been found, in need of repair but we would get by.

The Family Arrives

In the meantime, the family was living in Sweden, where both Maire and our thirteen-year-old son Olavi worked in a clothing factory. Kalervo and Rauha-Lilja attended a Swedish school, while Mirja, at six years of age, was not old enough to be in school. It had been arranged, however, that she could go along as an auditing pupil since she couldn't very well be left alone at home.

Thus mother and Olavi took care of the family's needs. Despite his young age, Olavi was like a father to the younger ones and took responsibility for them. Even as adults, a warm relationship continues between the eldest brother and his siblings. Olavi is more than a big brother to them. He had once taken his father's place that the others remember with gratitude.

Nevertheless, the family was in dire straits. When Christmas came, the children didn't buy toys with their gift money but rather food -yellow cheese. Maire was thrifty in her purchases as well, as an example to the children. Nothing was bought until it was first considered for its usefulness in Israel, to which the family continually and steadfastly aspired.

September 9, 1949 was a joyful day for all of us, when Maire and the children arrived on a Swedish freighter to Israel. The youngest child, Mirja, could hardly remember what her father looked like! "Father came and went and was away for such long periods of time, but now I can be with my father every day," were her first remarks. At the time of the family's arrival in Haifa, Olavi was fourteen, Kalervo twelve, Rauha-Lilja ten, and Mirja seven.

At the harbor, we loaded the luggage onto the back of a truck, together with the children, and headed for our new home. In the evening we thanked the Lord for our home, which enabled us at last to be together again after such a long separation. We lay the children to sleep on top of wooden crates and sighed with relief -although any stranger could have easily come in had they so desired, since the house still had no windows or doors.

Unbeknownst to us, the enemies were already in the house. The children had hardly fallen asleep when Rauha-Lilja, the eldest of our two daughters, cried out pitifully, "Father, an animal bit me on the nose!"

"Don't talk nonsense! You're just imagining." I said.

"But it bit me!" she insisted.

I turned on a flashlight and directed the beam around the room. I couldn't believe my eyes when I saw the gleaming eyes returning my stare. Rats, which had smelled the fresh "meat," had come into the house. One of these had indeed bitten Rauha-Lilja!

I quickly set a trap as I had done many times in the past when hunting for game birds in Finland. For a weight I used a table turned upside down, with stones on it and cheese for bait. A trigger-stick would spring the trap when the piece of cheese was touched.

We went back to sleep but it wasn't long before the table crashed down and squealing echoed through the house. I went to check, and of course I found the culprit. I threw it out the open window by its tail, and set the trap again. A bit later, a second rat flew into the yard. Thus it continued throughout the night. It may be that the others were able to catch some sleep while I was catching rats...

In the morning I told the boys, "Why don't you go outside to see how many rats there are under the window. Bury them so they don't begin to smell!"

The best catch for one night was sixteen rats.

The boys were rewarded for their work of killing rodents, so much for a mouse, a little more for a rat, a scorpion even more and a snake was the most, measured according to its length -not to be exaggerated!

Kalervo, the younger of the two boys, once shouted from the orchard, "Olavi, Olavi! Two hundred *mils* (0.5 Israeli pounds) are crawling in the orchard, come quickly to help me! Let's kill it! You can have half, you can have half!"

He had seen an adder, which he didn't even try to kill by himself. After the boys had finished the job, we found that the creature was 187 cm long. This was how our family began life together on the shores of the lake where our Saviour once lived.

Work Without Pay

Dr. Torrence had returned shortly before my family's arrival in Israel, bringing with him some hospital employees, including nurses and even a few midwives.

He must have been satisfied with my management of the hospital because he offered Olavi and myself jobs. "In such a large building there is much to do," he said.

That would be great, we thought, since money wasn't forthcoming for us from Finland, since Israel was not even considered a feasible place for

Christian work. We could thus earn a bit of income, which was at that time non-existent otherwise.

So Olavi and I went to work. We didn't even eat breakfast at the hospital but we arrived each morning on time, and worked a full day just like the others.

At the end of each week we waited for our wages so that we could buy food for the family.

But the doctor seemed to have forgotten completely about paying us! When we had worked there for about three months without getting food, drink, housing, or anything else, I summoned enough courage to tell the doctor, "Look here, Dr. Torrence! We ought to receive our wages already, since for three months we two men have worked faithfully for eight hours a day, six days a week. I have a family of six, four children and a wife. We need money for food and other necessities, just like everyone else."

"What's this? Wages? I thought you just wanted to help us," he responded innocently.

He acted as if he knew nothing about paying wages to us, so we had no more reason to continue working there. These were truly difficult times for us. For food, we picked wild sabra cactus fruit and dates from the palm trees in our yard. We caught fish from the lake and built a weir for them. Thus we survived from day to day. Sometimes it was very hard.

The doctor went to extremes in his stinginess. He asked me to find a Finnish nurse for the hospital and promised to pay for her airfare, so that they could quickly attain additional staff for the hospital.

I found them a Christian nurse but to this day, the airfare remains unpaid. At times, she would come to us and ask for a postage stamp in order to send a letter to Finland. "I haven't seen money for several months," she would say.

A Shame and a Disgrace

The hospital had a maternity ward of about forty beds. To save money, the nursery ward was closed at 10:00 P.M., left without a night nurse. The doors were reopened between 4:00 and 5:00 A.M. and now and then someone would check on the children, but there was no one on duty in their ward at night. "Who would try to steal children from there!?" was the doctor's comment when questioned. He saved the cost of a night nurse, if anyone ever actually received wages in that hospital.

This lack of supervision had serious consequences. At one point, it became necessary to install a new water system in the nursery. For this reason, a hole was made in the wall and left open for the work to be completed the following day. The fact that rats had multiplied tremendously throughout the land after the war was apparently not reason enough to close the hole. Our family alone had killed between four and five hundred of the creatures in our formerly deserted house before we "gained the upper hand."

A young Jewish woman from a kibbutz in the Jordan valley had just given birth to a baby boy at the hospital. The baby was born in good health. In the morning when the nurse came to see the newborns, she was horrified to discover this kibbutz baby about to choke from his crying. In place of a nose, there was only a gaping, bloody hole. The rats had come through the hole in the wall and eaten his nose!

The doctor received an urgent message, "Come quickly to settle with the baby's parents! Otherwise there will be a terrible scandal." But the doctor was not concerned. He just said, "What can we do about it? Accidents happen in all hospitals, do they not?"

The parents called the police and reporters to the scene. Newspapers spread the sensational news: "Rats even eat children's noses at Christian hospital!" The case was taken to court and huge sums were demanded in compensation.

The Scottish Mission Hospital was forced to pay heavily, including an annual air flight for the mother and the child to the United States in order to visit the world's best-known nose specialist. Each year a new artificial nose had to be made for him until he stopped growing.

Then, when the time came to renew the hospital's work permit, it was denied. An order came from the Ministry of Health to close the hospital and for its staff to be sent out of the country. Thus the work of the Scottish Mission Hospital ended, in 1959.

Today the Scottish Mission in Tiberias operates a tourist hostel and souvenir shop. They have an expansive property including several houses and a church. When I think of the sad fate of the hospital, James 5:4 always comes to mind, "Behold, the hire of the laborers who have reaped down your fields, which is of you kept back by fraud, crieth: and the cries of them which have reaped are entered into the ears of the Lord of sabaoth."

Sailors in Distress

New immigrants from India arrived in the village of Migdal. Some of them would visit us at our seaside home. Once, they stayed several hours. At the time we had a Finnish-made boat, with an outboard motor, given to us by the Mattsons. When it was time for our guests to go home I said to Maire, "It will be quite difficult for them to walk back to Migdal along the hot road, especially since they have small children with them. I think I'll take them home in our boat."

"It looks as if there's a bad storm on the lake. It wouldn't be wise to leave now," Maire objected.

"But we are on the calm end and the wind is blowing from west to east. There shouldn't be any danger," I answered.

"Be careful not to get caught in the storm," my wife insisted.

I took the family in the boat and we arrived safely to their village. As I turned to go back home, I noticed something strange in the middle of the lake. A mysterious object rose and fell on the waves. The Sea of Galilee is at its widest at that point, at about twelve kilometers. It was already afternoon and the storm was getting worse.

That isn't normal, I thought to myself, peering out into the sea. At that moment the Lord gave me an order: "Go there quickly!"

"How terrible!" I shouted. "To the middle of the lake?"

"Yes," the Lord said. "It's your duty."

I turned the boat with the wind and directed it to the middle of the lake. I was not mistaken: two people -a man and a woman- were in mortal danger. Their canoe was in a vertical position, rising and falling with the waves, the two desperate people clinging to it for dear life. The storm was all the while pushing them closer to the Syrian shore where an abundance of machine guns and soldiers were waiting to meet them. Often the Syrians would mercilessly kill Israelis who came too close. They would steal fishermen's nets and in every way make life insecure for them. If a Jew was captured, it would mean being killed or at best, imprisonment at Damascus. It was a fact that those who returned to Israel from Syrian captivity had endured cruel treatment or torture, some even went insane.

First I helped the wife into my boat, then the husband. "Let the canoe go," said the man, panting. "The main thing is that we are saved."

But I felt it was a pity to lose the canoe, so in spite of the strong waves rocking our boat, we emptied the canoe of water, lifted it up and made our way back to the western shore. Afraid that my gasoline would run out in the battle against the high waves, I prayed fervently for help from the Lord that we might make it back safely. Otherwise, Syria was our destiny, along with prison in Damascus or death, sooner or later!

The motor behaved faultlessly. As we approached the shore and the danger was over, I asked the couple where I should take them.

"We have a tent over there," the wife replied, pointing. "Our children are there."

I steered toward the sight of four children running from a tent towards their parents. I will never forget this reunion of mother and children, highlighted by endless tears and expressions of joy. It turned out that the family had come to spend their vacation on the shore of the lake. The parents had decided to go paddling a canoe along the lake and left their children alone for the time being.

The father extended his hand to me and said, "Thank you for saving our lives." He held my hand, squeezing it for a long time.

"Thank God that He sent me to help you in time," I said. "I am from Finland," I added. "I came to this country to distribute God's Word among the people."

This took place in October 1951.

Our Children at Risk

Evidently soldiers had for a time lived in our house, as here and there we found empty cartridge shells for machine guns. In fact, trash was scattered everywhere, which we collected and burned. In the yard, there was an old Arab stove which had no doubt been used to bake unleavened bread.

One day, Olavi and Rauha-Lilja were picking up trash and they decided to burn it in this old stove. Olavi was scraping out the ashes when the side of a hand grenade became visible. They threw themselves on the ground, thinking that they had set it off, and shouted a warning to the others. Thankfully, it did not explode.

Together we moved the ashes aside with caution, and found several other hand grenades as well. If the trash had simply been shoved into the stove and set on fire, the grenades would surely have exploded. Once again, God protected our family from a potentially terrible accident.

Poverty

The three years that we lived in the summer home on the shore of the Sea of Galilee were truly difficult times, testing us to the very limits of our strength. We couldn't get lumber at any price, nor were neither glass nor window screens available. So the wind blew right through our house.

Once every fifty years or so, it snows in Tiberias. One of those winters, it snowed. Inside the house the temperature was only five or six degrees Celsius since we had no heating. Miraculously, no one became ill not even with a common cold.

All food, even potatoes, were rationed, along with eggs, sugar and coffee. For fifteen years, the meat allowance per month per person was only three hundred grams, or ten and a half ounces.

Once I noticed a sack of whole-wheat flour in a shop. I asked for the price and since it wasn't too expensive, I bought the entire sixty-kilogram sack. This was a great help to us. It sufficed for making whole-wheat porridge for a long time. This was a very healthy source of food.

Christmas was coming. I earnestly asked for even a little change in our diet: *Dear Heavenly Father, give us some fish for Christmas*! To ask for a traditional Finnish Christmas ham would have been unthinkable.

I found some net material that we had brought with us and so I made a fish net. We swam out into the lake with it directly in front of our house. There was a warm spring close to the shore to which fish came in winter to spawn, but at that time we did not know of it.

On Christmas Eve we swam out to look at the fish trap. Already from a distance we could see the whole net shaking! "Get some pots quick," called the first swimmer to get there. "There are l-o-t-s of fish here!" We received the biggest catch of fish in our lives for our first Christmas in

Tiberias -sixty-five good-sized fish." Later our net got tangled up with someone else's and it was dragged away with it.

I decided to find out whether or not our manner of catching fish was even legal. It was then that I heard, "It is absolutely illegal and subject to a fine." I didn't dare tell the authorities that I had already fished with a weir-system, not to speak of the fact that my net had found its way to possibly even more fruitful territory.

I had written to a certain brother in Finland, telling him of our shortage of potatoes. One day, a ship company notified me of a shipment of one thousand kilograms of potatoes soon to arrive from Finland! A short while after the notice, another letter came from the public welfare office saying, "One thousand kilos of potatoes are on their way to you. These will be distributed to the general public. In due time you will receive compensation for them."

We began to wait for this large potato shipment. It was delayed a long while, at least a couple of months. I often wondered where it could have gone astray, since it didn't arrive at its destination.

One Sunday morning while we were at the worship service, a large truck appeared in front of our house. The driver came inside and told us that the potatoes had arrived, and demanded payment for the transportation costs.

"I have a dump truck," he said. "I can dump the entire load onto your yard."

"Do that," I agreed. "We can move them into storage from there."

We continued the service. After it was over, we went to look at the potatoes, only to be met by an awful stench. Almost the entire load was rotten! It was like a manure pile at our gate. *No wonder the welfare office allowed the whole load to be brought to us*! I thought to myself.

Nevertheless, we made use of what we could. If even the slightest part of a potato could be salvaged we did so. The rest was dumped into a pit that we dug in the orchard. The sun dried out the pieces that we had cut out, and the entire house smelled like rotten potatoes! But for several months we had plenty of dried potatoes. The journey had obviously been too long and there had been a delay in their delivery. In any case, the sender had meant well.

A Wolf in Sheep's Clothing

I received a letter from someone in Finland. She informed me of her daughter who was on the way to Jerusalem. She asked me to help find housing for her and to assist her in getting acquainted with life in Israel.

I knew it to be difficult to find lodging in Israel, particularly in Jerusalem. The girl came first to our place and then together we went to look for accommodations. I suddenly recalled the large American organization I'd been to before and so we went to ask the pastor whether he would have a vacant room in which the Finnish student could live.

"Yes, that would be fine," the pastor replied. "And if the girl would be willing to help a couple of hours a day washing dishes she does not have to pay rent."

"Good! Settle this matter between the two of you then," I said and left her there.

About two months later, I had a strong urge to visit my young Finnish friend. I left for Jerusalem immediately.

The girl looked peculiar when we met. When I openly wondered why this was so, she said, "Let's go out for a walk."

We went to a nearby park and sat down on a bench. She burst into tears, crying hopelessly.

"What in the world has happened to you?" I asked. "Has a close relative passed away or is someone deathly ill, or are you ill yourself?"

"No, it's much worse than that..."

"Tell me please, dear girl, or I won't be able to even try and help you!" I encouraged.

She exclaimed, "You have no idea what kind of house you brought me to live in!"

Suddenly I remembered the dream I had had about the devil and the giant snake. "Tell me the whole truth immediately, no matter what. I want to know."

"The pastor asked me whether or not I was a believer. 'Yes', I told him. 'I was born again a few years ago'. Then he asked me if I had received the baptism of the Holy Spirit yet. 'No, I haven't received it yet', I replied. He told me that he has the kind of gift that when he prays on behalf of people, they receive the baptism of the Holy Spirit, and he suggested that we take care of this matter after the meeting. Then he prayed for me but nothing happened."

This man had an unusual gift of eloquence. People were downright enthralled by his manner and many would come to hear him even from a great distance. Several came forward at the meetings wanting to be saved, but it was strange that they experienced no change in their lives. They did not remain in the faith; there was no lasting fruit.

"Once after a meeting, the two of us were left alone," the girl continued. "The pastor grabbed me and began to fondle me wildly. 'I want to come to your room this evening,' he said. I tore myself loose from his grip and ran to my room but I didn't have time to lock the door. He was right behind me. I managed to kick him out the door and even to try and lock it but then my strength gave out...."

While the girl sat beside me crying, many things became clear to me. I told her, "You must not stay one more day in that house. Now I understand the dream I had some time ago. You will now go and pack your things. In one hour I will come in a taxi to the front of the house. In the meantime, I'll go and look for another place for you."

We did just that, and for her this was the end of a traumatic episode. But unfortunately, this kind of incident was not the last one.

A certain Messianic believer (Ms. L.W.) had belonged in Switzerland to a denomination that knew nothing of the baptism of the Holy Spirit. She left Jerusalem to visit her native country and the Lord filled her there with His Holy Spirit. She then joined the Zurich Pentecostal congregation. As she was preparing to return to Israel, someone told her of an English pastor who lives in a large house in Jerusalem. "Since you know five languages, you can be a big help to him as an interpreter."

About the same time, another sister, Ms. E.C., was sent from London to Jerusalem by the same Swiss organization and so these two women went to live in the house from which the Finnish girl had left.

Having heard this, I had a strong urge to warn these sisters of the possibility of unpleasant surprises. I did visit them but after realizing that both women were already quite enchanted by this pastor, I was quite unable to say anything about the unfortunate possibilities. So I did what I knew to do in such a situation: Pray! *Lord, You warn and protect them since I cannot*, I would plead.

I came back home in peace and sent them a letter with the words, "If for some reason you should sometime need a peaceful place to live, you can come to us at the shore of the Galilee to rest. The Lord has given us a large home and you don't need to pay anything for your stay."

One day a telegram arrived. "Is your offer still valid? Wire a reply."

I sent the reply, "Welcome!"

On the evening of the same day I met the sisters at the bus station and brought them to our home. Maire was just preparing tea and refreshments when both sisters, adult women, one of them a doctor of philosophy, burst out in bitter tears, just as the Finnish girl had done when I met her in Jerusalem.

We didn't say anything, didn't ask anything, but rather took care of them as little children. At times they went out to swim and we would feed them as best we could. One evening a week later, L.W. asked me, "Do you know why that girl from Finland left that place?"

"Yes, I know. She told me everything." I responded.

"We had to leave for this same reason," was her only comment.

The women stayed with us for a little while, until they were able to buy a caravan mobile home. They lived in it for some time in Tiberias and then they moved to Mt. Carmel. Together with these two sisters we worked for over twenty years distributing Bibles.

A few years ago, L.W. fell and seriously hurt herself. She was taken by ambulance to the airport and flown to Switzerland. She recovered, but soon later she retired, as she was already about seventy years of age. For over forty years she was involved in God's work in this land. The English sister, E.C., has stayed by her side. They live currently in a small village in Switzerland.

Chapter 12

The Bible Work Begins

Shipments of Three Hundred Copies

Our work of distributing Bibles began in Tiberias in 1956. First, we rented rooms from the Scottish Mission. These memoirs have actually been recorded from down in their wine cellar. It serves well not only as a bomb shelter but also as a cool place in the summer and a pleasantly warm one in winter.

God knows all things in advance. He doesn't need to make any guesses about anything in the future, as humans do. God knew the fate of the Scottish Mission Hospital already in 1944 when I He said to me, "I want to open a new 'station' on the shores of the Sea of Galilee and to appoint you as the 'stationmaster'."

Immigrants from about one hundred countries throughout the world have come to Israel. A true mix of tongues is found in the land, even newspapers are available in over twenty different languages. Hebrew is of course the main language.

The basic textbook in schools is the Hebrew Bible. It is of course highly respected, taught daily and given an important place in all aspects of education. Schools do not provide books or other supplies for the students. Thus it was only natural that we first provide the schools with Hebrew Bibles which also contain the New Testament.

Dr. Myron Sackett of the USA helped us. He purchased Hebrew Bibles from the London Bible Society that he would send us in shipments of three hundred.

In our work of distribution to the schools, we would first approach the school administrator and ask whether they had enough Bibles. At one school in the Upper Galilee, when I asked how many students there were in the school, the reply was "about three hundred."

"Do you have enough Bibles?" I inquired further.

The answer was shocking. "We have about twenty or thirty. The students take turns borrowing them from each other. There is a great shortage because they aren't even sold anywhere."

"We have some Bibles in the car. We could give you some of them." I took a sample from my pocket and said, "As you can see, the New Testament is included in the ones we have."

"Better yet," he answered. "They can learn about that as well!"

Thus began the work of Bible distribution in Israel.

Opposition at Customs

There are zealous Ultra-Orthodox Jews in this country. Some were not pleased to discover that the Bibles we had given to the schools included the New Testament. They took action and passed a bill that forbade the importing of Hebrew Bibles that contain the New Testament. We had no idea this had happened.

The next shipment of three hundred Bibles arrived some time later. We received a letter informing us of their arrival, with instructions to "come clear the matter and to see that the papers are in order." When I realized our dilemma, I prayed to the Lord and asked Him for wisdom in handling this new problem. The Lord answered, "First of all, don't go to the department where the Bibles are being held. Go instead to a higher customs official!"

It is true that in Israel, it is always preferable to go "straight to the top." I have found that among the ones in the top ranks there are a few secret Nicodemus-believers who understand matters differently from their subordinates.

So I went to the man in charge. I explained that we give Bibles to schools free of charge. This new regulation had been put into effect without my having been informed. Therefore I had not even known that I should have applied for a special permit. I asked him, "Is such a law really in existence?"

He looked through his papers and said, "That law came into effect four weeks ago."

I replied, "Our Bibles left London six weeks ago, two weeks before this new law was passed. I believe that I have the right to get the Bibles from customs without further ado."

He inspected the papers that had been sent from London and agreed with me. "Yes! You are absolutely right. Let's go downstairs and find those Bibles."

It seems he intended to give me the Bibles without further questions but we were met by an Orthodox Jew, complete with a black hat and curly sidelocks. He was ecstatic, having actually caught hold of a live missionary! "Why are you bringing such books into the country? We don't need Bibles with the New Testament. Your books have been confiscated and they will never be released. Furthermore, this type of Bible will no longer be permitted to be brought here."

I listened politely. What else could I do in such a situation? But I did notice that the customs official looked a little embarrassed. He remained quiet but when we left the department, he turned to me and said, "I have the authority to release those Bibles if you will, as a formality, pay a small fine. Perhaps five Israeli pounds will do."

"That would suit me just fine," I said.

We went into his office. I gave him the agreed sum and he handed me a receipt that read, "Fine paid. The Bibles must be released." With a friendly smile, he said, "Show this paper and you will get your books."

Just as I was about to go out the door, the phone rang. I heard the official answer the voice at the other end, "It's too late! He has paid his fine and I have written the release order. The matter is closed."

Downstairs, the man was ready to have a fit. But he had no choice but to do his duty.

Not long after this adventure, word came from customs again. "We have three hundred Bibles here! Please come to take care of this matter as soon as possible."

I was reminded of the man not particularly favorably disposed to our interests. Like a chained lion, he would surely be in a rage if he saw me again. So I prayed, *Dear Heavenly Father! Have mercy and help me so that I don't need to go to Haifa at all, but that I could get those Bibles some other way.*

The Lord said, "You don't have to go to Haifa. Do you remember that the Israeli Minister of Justice is an open-minded man, a member of the Liberal Party, who now and again clashes with the Orthodox? Write him a letter! Offer these Bibles as gifts for the Israeli prison libraries. Surely they have reason to read God's Word and at the same time learn Hebrew."

I did as I was told. The Minister's reply was encouraging, with thanks for the valuable gift. He urged me to get in touch with the chief director of prisons. The prison director was very friendly and he also thanked me for the gift. The solution was simple: "We will take care of transportation of the Bibles from customs. Sign your name on this form please."

Sometimes it may seem as if we are playing chess with the devil but as soon as we ask Him who is on our side for wisdom, the victory is ours!

My Friend the Rabbi "Saves the Day"

I was about to leave on vacation to Finland when I received news of a third shipment of three hundred Bibles. This time I was reminded of my friend H.B., whom I had met on the ship coming to the country. He had promised to help me if I was ever in difficulty. So I went to see him in Jerusalem. We met in his study.

"How is your Bible distribution work coming along?" the friendly old man asked.

"I have been able to get the last two shipments of Bibles through customs. The first we gave to schools and the second to prisons. Now a third shipment is here and I don't know how I can get it out. This is my reason for turning to you for the assistance we spoke about on the ship to Israel."

He immediately took the matter into his care. Grabbing the phone, he began frantically dialing numbers. I wondered whom he was calling.

Then I heard, "Is this the minister of education? Listen. H.B. speaking. Do we have a law that forbids God's Word from coming into our country? If so, we live in conditions comparable to those in communist countries! I have a friend who is doing wonderful work, distributing Hebrew Bibles to schools and prison libraries. It is a downright shame and scandal that such a law has been passed! Besides, it's unfortunate because he is about to leave on vacation to Scandinavia. He may have to explain to his friends that we confiscate Bibles in Israel. Take care of this matter quickly! I am sending him to you."

The next thing I knew, I was holding a piece of paper on which he had recorded the time of my appointment with the minister of education. And that was not all! He asked me to send him forty or fifty copies when I received the Bibles. "I will give some to the Hebrew University library and some to the professors here. It is a good thing that we can receive the type of Bible that contains the New Testament. These have not been nor will they ever be printed here."

He added, "We have a Bible study group. I will write down the names and addresses of a few of the members. Could you send each one a copy by mail?"

"I'd be glad to do so," I replied.

"Keep these names to yourself. This is rather confidential information which I'm sure you understand," he asked.

I went straight to the Ministry of Education. After being inspected for possession of weapons or explosives, the guards directed me to the distinguished gentleman.

He greeted me with the words, "I am sorry that you have had problems with those Bibles. Do you have the customs documents with you?"

I showed them to him and then he said, "Sign your name on this form authorizing the Ministry of Education to take the Bibles out of customs. They will be mailed to your Tiberias post box within two days. Have a pleasant trip home!"

The ordeal was over. Two days later, we received the Bibles as promised. Fifty of them were immediately packaged for the dean of the university and several smaller packages made their way to the homes of Israel's upper-class citizens.

The Haifa customs clerk was upset again, upon the arrival of a third "illegal" shipment. He reported to his headquarters that something would need to be done, "since those 'damned missionaries' had been able to continue bringing Hebrew Bibles with New Testaments into the country, even without an import permit."

The Orthodox Party is very active in their mission. Although they make up only fifteen percent of the population, they hold a disproportionate amount of power in Parliament. They control, among others, the Ministry of Interior, the Ministry of Religious Affairs, the Ministry of Social Affairs.

This matter of Bibles was brought to the attention of the *Knesset*, the Israeli Parliament. When the chairman met with the board of members, he read a letter which outlined the crisis: "How do you explain a situation that allows missionaries to continue to import into the country Bibles that contain the New Testament even though there are clear regulations which forbid the granting of import licenses for this purpose?"

The question might have resulted in an extended debate. But the chairman objected to the manner in which the issue was presented. He closed the matter, saying, "This letter has not been brought forth in accordance with established procedures, via the legislative secretary's office. It will not be discussed at this time." The matter was dropped and it has not been discussed since.

The name of that chairman was at the head of my list to whom such Bibles had been sent. He was a brave man as well as a friend of Finland! He had been in Finland in 1905, at a Zionist conference. When a new street was built in Tel Aviv, he suggested the name Helsinki Street. The reason for his favorable attitude was likely due to the fact that Helsinki welcomed the Zionists whereas nowhere in Russia, for example, would such a conference have been permitted.

A Large-Scale Printing Job

Unfortunately, the London Bible shipments came to an end. Dr. Sackett asked them if they could print more, since these Bibles continued to be in great demand. All the schools in Israel had need of them.

The Bible Work Begins

"Could you print fifty-thousand copies for us, and what would this cost?" he asked them.

The director of the Bible Society deliberated a few moments and then replied, "They will cost three dollars apiece and it will take two years to print them."

Dr. Sackett wrote me with this response and asked me for advice. I replied, "My dear friend, do not make such an agreement! The printing time is much too long and the price too high." Then I told him of my contact in Sweden, Florentius Hallzon, the publisher of *Hemmets Van* and a great friend of Israel. Through advertising in his newspaper, he had once collected a million dollars for new immigrants to Israel and he is the one who had paid for my first trip from London to Israel. So I urged Dr. Sackett to turn to him, and I assured him that I would write to Hallzon in advance, informing him of our need.

He took my advice and traveled to see my old Swedish friend. Hallzon had an answer ready for him. "We are very happy that you wish to give God's Word to the people of Israel. The price will be two dollars apiece with an additional five thousand copies free of charge. We shall begin the work tomorrow morning." This was certainly a different kind of offer from the one received from England.

It was in 1956 that this enormous printing job began. Dr. Sackett was to come to Israel to show me a sample copy of the new edition but just then the Sinai War broke out. His passport had been stamped "Not valid for the Middle East." He told Hallzon that he couldn't take a sample copy to Syväntö as agreed, since his passport forbade travel to Israel. However, Ingemar Hallzon, the publisher's eldest son who is now continuing in his father's footsteps, came instead. He told me of the printing going on in Sweden. I wondered how we would get them into the country and how soon could we get them distributed.

I was honestly somewhat worried. How had I dared to order such a large number of Bibles considering the trouble I had found myself in on previous occasions, with much smaller shipments! Then I remembered that there was soon to be a large-scale conference of the various Christian communities in Jerusalem. Our son Olavi would be there, as he was working for an American organization at the time. We could go there and ask all of these colleagues to distribute our Bibles!

In Prestigious Company

At the conference, we found ourselves sitting at a long table. The chairman was the presiding Anglican archbishop in the Middle East. He sat at the head of the table, gold cross on his chest. I asked for permission to speak and explained that we had fifty thousand copies of the Hebrew Bible ready for shipment in Sweden. I introduced the son of the director of the printing press who had with him a sample copy. We were asking those present how many of them would like to cooperate with us in distributing the Bibles among the people of Israel.

I put the newly printed Bible into the hands of the Archbishop. He looked at it, turning some pages. He noticed the name of the printer, Evangeliipress, Orebro Sweden.

"What kind of a press is this?" he asked. "We don't distribute Bibles from any private publishing firms, only those of the British and foreign Bible Societies. In this task we don't need any private enterprises. Our Bible Society has to this day handled this country's Bible needs and it will continue to do so. Besides, it is not a proper distribution method to give out Bibles as gifts. Anyone who wishes to read it should buy a Bible for himself from the Bible Society bookshop just like the rest of us."

Afterwards, he passed the sample around the table. A strange, heavy feeling came over the meeting. Not much was said. When the sample had been circulated among the twenty-five delegates, I was again allowed to have the floor. I said, "I don't want to waste any more of your precious time. I just want to ask one question: Is there anyone in this group who would like to distribute Bibles if we get them into the country?"

Two people raised their hands. One was the Finnish Evangelical Lutheran delegate. The other was an American pastor. Only two brave ones in the group dared to announce their interest.

The meeting left a "bad taste in my mouth." Thinking seriously about this development, we returned to Tiberias. I told the brother from Sweden, "Ten kilometers from Tiberias there is a prophet of the Lord. Let's go and visit him."

We went to see Reverend Rex Andrews, a seventy-five year old servant of the Lord from America who lived in Poria Elite. He was among the first ones to have received the baptism of the Holy Spirit in Los Angeles in 1905. I told him of the sad events in Jerusalem. After a few minutes, he turned to pray and then he received the following word of knowledge through the Holy Spirit: "I gave this task to you! Don't peek around, don't look to others and don't wait for help from people. I, the Lord, will take care of this matter. Go forward in faith!"

I then understood that it was useless to look for help from other people. The best helper is the Heavenly Father Himself.

Ingemar Hallzon returned to Sweden and asked me to report back what we were going to do with the Bibles. I began to ponder this question. Then the Lord reminded me that years ago when I had been a railroad employee, I had taken a course in international postal regulations. I had passed the examination with high marks. I remembered that Israel belongs to the International Postal Union, the headquarters of which are in Switzerland.

The Lord said, "Bring those books into the country by mail!"

The only thing needed was names and addresses! The International Postal Union officially guarantees that in all countries that belong to the union, the mail must reach its destination. If it does not arrive, the country is put on a blacklist. In such cases, the mail has to be marked, "At the risk of the sender."

In those days, all communist countries were on the blacklist and the union could not guarantee delivery of the mail sent to these countries. In no way did Israel want to be put on the blacklist!

Chapter 13

A New Phase in the Work

Bibles in the Post

So it was only a question of getting as many names and addresses as possible. Once a week, a package weighing three kilos could be sent to each address.

I went first to the Nazareth EMMS Hospital where the head doctor, Dr. Bathgate, was our good friend. I explained to him the situation, of our need for persons willing to receive packages in the mail. "We will come to retrieve them ourselves and distribute them where needed," I told him. As an answer, he put into my hands the entire list of staff members, between forty and fifty names.

Next, Aili Havas of the Finnish Evangelical Lutherans provided a number of names.

From my own addresses I compiled a list of Arab and messianic believers.

At the end I had about three hundred addresses. I sent these to Sweden with a note asking them to send one package per week to each person.

Thus Bibles began to flow into the land. We were busy collecting them from each address since they were spread out throughout the country.

It became essential for us to have a vehicle but these were very expensive also because of a customs fee of three hundred percent!

The "Bible-Mobile"

The problem was solved but not without a few difficulties. Our son Kalervo was about to be married to Meri -- in Helsinki. Meri's father was a Jew in Finland and through Dean H.B.'s help, she was able to get an immigrant visa to Israel. New immigrants do not pay such high customs fees for vehicles. Thus the new couple could purchase a Volkswagen in Hamburg, on their way to Israel, and it could be registered in Meri's name.

I handled matters at this end. The customs agent who handled Kalervo and Meri's belongings took care of the papers needed for the port at Haifa, including a release permit for the car. He said nothing to my comment that Meri didn't have a driver's license except, "it shouldn't be a problem for a man to drive his wife's car?"

It was the last day of the year when the agent came to see us, with a thick bundle of papers, saying, "Nothing more is needed except your daughter-in-law's driver's license!"

"Didn't I tell you in the beginning that she doesn't have one? She has never driven a car!"

"That's really too bad!" he exclaimed. "I didn't pay any attention to this question although you may very well have mentioned it. We cannot do anything about it if she doesn't have her license. And that is not all, a new ruling requires her to have had her license for at least a year and a half before immigrating. I won't even try to solve this. It's simply impossible. Here are the papers. Take care of it yourself. The case is closed." With these words, he left.

I stood perplexed for a moment. I looked at the clock. It was fifteen minutes to two o'clock on December 31. I had a quarter of an hour before the customs office would close. Turning to the Lord, I prayed, *Please help me quickly! This is concerning Your car and Your business. The Bibles are scattered throughout the country and they must be collected. You have promised: 'Call upon me in the day of trouble: I will deliver thee, and thou shalt glorify me'* (Psalms 50:15).

I cried, *This is my day of trouble! I have fifteen minutes left!*

Then I told the young people who were with me at the time, "On your knees quickly before the Lord, so that we can get the car out of customs!"

I felt prompted by the Lord to go as quickly as possible to the chief customs official and to tell him the whole situation, hiding nothing!

I didn't have the slightest idea where his office was located and I didn't know his name. The building was huge, three stories high with offices on two sides. Suddenly I noticed a door with a sign, "Director of Customs."

With my heart pounding, I knocked at the door and stepped in, having heard a friendly voice inviting me to enter. Nervously, I thought of what I should say and how I should begin to present my case.

But I didn't need to say anything. As I stepped inside, the friendly director rose from his desk and extended his hand to me, saying "Mr. Syväntö from Tiberias? It's good to see you again after such a long time! Do you remember me from the time when you lived in Dr. Heart's summer home on the shore of the Sea of Galilee? You let me swim in that warm spring along your beach and you offered me all sorts of refreshments. Your daughters were great divers and swimmers as well. Are you still living there?"

"No, I haven't lived there for about ten years." At that moment I couldn't actually recall this genial gentleman. We tried to be hospitable to guests and friendly to everyone who came to visit us.

"How nice that on this last day of the year you came to greet me! Or did you have some business as well?"

"Yes, I do," I replied. He asked me to sit down. I related to him our situation: "You asked me what I am doing now. Our whole family is working toward one goal. We are distributing God's Word among your people. But we have had great difficulty since we didn't get a permit to import Bibles to Israel. Now they have to be brought in by mail. As it stands, these packages have come to various parts of the country and we need an automobile to collect them. Otherwise nothing will come of our work. We had hoped that for this purpose we would be able to get the vehicle that was registered in our daughter-in-law's name but the agent said that she would have to have a driver's license that has been in effect for at least a year and a half."

"Those are indeed the present regulations regarding this matter. She does need to have her own driver's license," the director agreed.

"I came to see you to ask whether the automobile could be brought into the country in spite of these regulations. As a family we can get along without a car but the Bible work will suffer if we don't have one. We don't have any organization to support us. We are just an ordinary family, wanting to spread the Word of God among these people. We don't receive a regular salary; we have to pay for gasoline and other needs ourselves. And we give out all the Bibles as <u>free</u> gifts."

I looked at the director of customs straight in the eye. He folded his hands, bowed his head and apparently prayed. I did the same across the desk from him, *Lord, be merciful and allow the automobile to come through*!

After a few moments the director opened his eyes, raised his head and said, "It is truly a great deed you are doing by giving our people the Word of God as a free gift. We have here the problem of one missing driver's license, do we not? Do you have your son's driver's license with you?"

I gave it to him. "We'll write that number on the documents but don't speak much about it to others. Good luck and blessings to you in your work. Happy New Year!"

That was a conversation worth two million marks. It turned out that the automobile rolled along the roads of Israel for the next sixteen years. Since it was purchased, the motor was replaced once and its mileage reached four hundred thousand kilometers. Today we have a new vehicle but it had a different price: twenty thousand Finnish marks (per exchange rate in 1999).

The Archbishop's Mistake

The archbishop who had boasted about his own country's Bible Society being able to take care of Bible needs without the help of "private societies" apparently did not succeed in his endeavors.

In this country there is only one paper plant, located in Hadera. Someone had complained that this factory did not keep the Sabbath. Black smoke rose from its chimney even on the Sabbath day. The chief rabbi called the chief engineer at the plant, saying, "We are now in Israel and one must not light a fire on the Sabbath. You are desecrating the Sabbath. This kind of activity must stop once and for all."

To this the engineer replied, "That which is coming out of the chimney is not smoke. We have a paper factory that means we do not burn paper, we make it! Furthermore, this is the only paper mill in this country. That which rises from the chimney is a poisonous gas. It has to be released into the air, otherwise our plant will become a gas chamber and you know what has happened in gas chambers. It is totally impossible for us to operate in any other way. There are no alternatives. The chemical process is continual and the poisonous gas must be released into the air. The paper pulp will spoil if we don't continue doing this."

The chief rabbi became angry since his word was not obeyed and he declared all products from the Hadera paper mill non-kosher. No religious literature was allowed to be printed on non-kosher paper.

No one was therefore able to print religious literature in Israel for two and a half years, neither the Jews nor the Bible Society. But we had a great demand for Bibles and we were able to get them via our continual stream of mail from Sweden. Kalervo drove five days a week, collecting the packages and distributing them to those who asked for the Scriptures. Working with him were the two sisters who had sought refuge in our home when they escaped from Jerusalem.

Due to these unfortunate circumstances, the Bible Society began to have a real need for Bibles. At great cost, they hired a lawyer who requested an import permit on their behalf. The permit was not granted.

It took two and a half years before an agreement was reached between the paper mill and the chief rabbi. A rabbi-inspector was sent to the site to make sure that no fire had been lit and that only Arabs were working on the Sabbath. Only then was the ban lifted and the rabbi's blessing granted to the paper mill.

A year after the re-opening of the mill, the Bible Society received their order of ten thousand copies.

Out of curiosity, five years after the prestigious conference in Jerusalem where my offer of Bibles had been rejected, I inquired how many Bibles had been sold by the Bible Society. I was told one thousand eight hundred copies. During that same period, through the mercy of God, we had distributed more than one hundred thousand copies. It seems that "private societies" were indeed needed.

Mr. Hallzon and Dr. Sackett wanted to make known the fact that we were distributing such large numbers of Bibles. When I heard about it, I told them, "Dear friends! Please don't do that! We have enough problems in this country as it is. We plan to continue this work and we mustn't breathe a word about how many have already been distributed."

A Trouble-Making Director of Postal Services

One day I was horrified to read in the newspaper that one of the Orthodox Party, B.M., had been appointed director of postal services. He was an energetic-looking man, about fifty years of age. I guessed that our struggle would soon get worse and so it did.

The next thing I knew, a uniformed policeman came to our door and asked me to come with him to the station. Two officers were assigned to the questioning. They began to press me for details about the Bible ministry, in Hebrew.

It occurred to me that I could best get out of this dilemma by explaining myself directly to the chief of police. Our eldest daughter and the chief's daughter were schoolmates. On his 50th birthday, Rauha-Lilja had painted a beautiful floral design on a vase for her friend's father. So we knew each other, at least by name. I sighed in my heart of hearts that the Lord would give me wisdom about how to make my suggestion.

I showed them my passport and said, "I am a Finnish citizen, don't you gentlemen realize what the law says about questioning foreigners? It is always to be conducted in the language that the one questioned knows best. I know Finnish, Swedish and English. I do not intend to answer your questions in any other language. This is my legal right."

The police were embarrassed for they knew only Hebrew. So they called their boss and asked him whether this was indeed the case, concerning my rights. "Of course," the chief answered. "Don't you know English?" he asked them.

"No, we know Hebrew only," they responded.

Of course I understood for the most part what I was being asked but my reaction was an ideal way to come in contact with the chief himself!

He answered, "Tell Mr. Syväntö that I will come shortly to take care of this matter."

My plan worked. He greeted me amiably and asked me to step into his office. It was I who began to question him. "Have you, the chief of police, launched an attack against us?"

"By no means!" he replied.

"Then where does this investigation originate?" I asked.

"It's that new director of postal services."

"I thought so!" I exclaimed.

He pulled from his desk drawer a memorandum and showed it to me. "This is dated December 15 but I didn't want to disturb you at Christmastime. It has been sitting in my desk for a couple of months and now I felt I should bother you a little, with these questions."

Of course the man was only doing his job. I asked him, "What is the crime of which I am being accused?"

"The director of postal services is upset by the fact that in spite of a law against it, large numbers of Hebrew Bibles which include the New Testament have been brought to the country. He has received news of at least one hundred thousand copies imported in a clearly organized fashion. The tracks lead to you. You are the organizer."

"All of this is true," replied. "I have arranged the importing and distribution of the Bibles. Only the figure is not exact. To date, six printings totaling one hundred and eighty-five thousand copies have come to this country."

"This issue really does concern astronomical figures!" shouted the chief. "You are accused of illegal, extensive business dealings without a business license. Furthermore, the state requires a ten-percent sales tax on all those books that you have sold in this country. I have heard that no sales tax has been paid. Do you keep accurate accounts of your business, including the payment of taxes?"

I could honestly never have guessed that I would run into such a surprising situation. But God is not met by surprises. The Lord had told me from the very beginning, before we really got going with the ministry, to order three rubber stamps and to send them to Sweden. They were to be engraved with the words, "GIFT, NOT FOR SALE" in both English and Hebrew. In addition, each package was to have a glued-on label that reads, "THIS PACKAGE CONTAINS A FREE GIFT WITHOUT ANY COMMERCIAL VALUE."

Thus I was freed from this predicament. If I had not had this proof how could I have even attempted to claim that I hadn't sold any Bibles? It would have been a serious offense to do business and to refuse to pay taxes.

I showed him one of the Bibles and a package in which they come into the country. "We give all the Bibles as gifts. We have never sold a single book nor do we intend to do so. I know full well that in Russia and in other communist countries, one cannot distribute Bibles but does Israel belong to this same category? Is this a democratic country in practice, or in theory only?"

Having seen the labels with his own eyes, and having been shown the "goods" that were not for sale, he exclaimed, "For goodness' sake! You are doing a fantastic service in giving us God's Word free of charge. This case is now closed. Continue your work, and may God bless you in all of your activities!"

The Battle for Bibles Continues

Suddenly the Bibles stopped coming. The director of postal services was not satisfied with the results of the inquiry. In fact, he was more agitated than ever and he gave an order to confiscate all of our Bible packages.

Someone told me of a famous attorney who worked in Jerusalem. He would surely be able to appeal the illegal confiscation order. I went to him, explained the situation and asked if he would take the case.

The answer was simply "No." He explained, "I will not take this kind of case no matter what the fee, even though you are in the right and the confiscation order is wrong. It would ruin my reputation and my career if it became known that I took 'a missionary case' -even if I should win it. I'm sorry, Mr. Syväntö."

This is what happens to us when we rely on our own wisdom. I returned home with no answers and with considerably less in my pocket after paying the lawyer's consultation fee. It was a good reason to pray, so I turned to the Lord and said *Dear Heavenly Father! I made a mistake in 'trusting my flesh' when I went to see that attorney. Please give me clear instructions. I promise to struggle on behalf of this ministry to my dying day, but the Bibles must come through for the people. I will really try to obey You but please give me clear orders, showing how to proceed.* I also asked for a quote from the Bible confirming His instructions.

The Lord answered with a remarkable verse: "This kind goeth not out but by prayer and fasting" (Matthew 17:21). I took that as a clear word and direct advice from God. I understood that the issue involved a struggle against the powers of darkness, which do not want people to read the Word of God.

I took the advice seriously and fasted for ten days. I even sent an intercessory prayer request to Finland that the confiscation rule be reversed. One night as I was awake during the early morning hours, praying quietly in my bed, I experienced a mysterious brightness in my soul. It was for me a sign that we had gained a victory in the spirit world.

I felt the Lord urging me to type a letter to the attorney general with copies to the president, prime minister, minister of justice and director of postal services. In the letter I informed his Honor that the director of postal services had confiscated some international personal mail. I told him of my intention to send a protest of this action to the International Postal Union in Geneva that would result in an international scandal for Israel. Here is an excerpt from my letter:

> The most distressing part of this affair is having to testify to the fact that the object being confiscated is the Word of God, the Bible. If this ruling is not repealed, people throughout the world will be amazed to hear that Israel, by confiscating Bibles in its own land, has sided with the communist countries.

I ended the letter with a reminder of wise old Gamaliel's words before the Great Council: "I say unto you, Refrain from these men, and let them alone: for if this counsel or this work be of men, it will come to naught: But if it be of God, ye cannot overthrow it; lest haply ye be found even to fight against God!" (Acts 5:38-39). With these words I presented my request to the minister of justice that the confiscation order be declared unlawful.

Because I have a permanent visa, I dared to write such a bold letter. To be sure that the letters would not simply land in a wastebasket, I sent them as registered mail. About one month later, I received the following reply from the attorney general:

A New Phase in the Work

```
                    מדינת ישראל
                    STATE OF ISRAEL

MINISTRY OF JUSTICE                            משרד המשפטים

                              Jerusalem, March 27, 1961
                                    932/7/5
Mr. K.O. Syvanto,
P.O. Box 86,
Tiberias.

Dear Sir,
                                        (Bibles)
           I have been informed that the books
   which were the subject of complaint in your
   letter dated 13.2.1961 have been released.
           I regret and apologise for any in-
   convenience caused you in this matter.
                              Yours faithfully,

                              [signature]
                              G. Hasid
                              Deputy State Attorney
                              (transl...)
```

I was truly pleased with this decision and sent a letter of thanks to the minister of justice, expressing my joy and gratitude that the head of Israel's Supreme Court is a righteous and law-abiding man. I added, "And as you continue in this upright way, God's blessing will also continue to be upon your actions."

Thus the battle was over and our work was allowed to continue.

But another surprise was on the way!

Another Roadblock

Our American friends, Mr. and Mrs. M.T.C. Davis, promised to pay for the printing of twenty thousand Hebrew New Testaments. The work was to be done in Tel Aviv, at Israel's best publishing house. Unfortunately, this same publishing firm printed all of the stamps, in addition to other materials, for the postal service.

This was the "difficult situation" which the manager of the publishing company called to explain to me. The director of postal services had discovered that we were also one of their customers and as a result threatened to withdraw all of their orders. The manager asked me: "What should we do now?"

"I don't want to create any problems for you," I replied. "Let's postpone our request for now and see what happens in the meantime."

"I'm glad that you understand," he replied, relieved.

"Take care of the problem as you see best, so that you won't suffer any financial loss because of us," I said to him. He thanked me with sincerity and the problem was abandoned for the time being.

I then went to the Lord and said, *Listen! That director of postal services is still trying to prevent us! Your Word says, 'Faith cometh by hearing, and hearing by the Word of God' (Romans 10:17). Those yet-unprinted Bibles are absolutely necessary for this nation. It is no one other than the devil himself opposing the printing. I leave this entire problem and its solution in Your hands. Do what You see best, but please have mercy so that those New Testaments can be printed, and quickly!*

This is how I left it. What else could I have done? But then there was an unexpected turn of events.

About two weeks after the publisher's phone call and our postponing of the printing, he called again. "Did you listen to this morning's news report?" he asked.

"No, was there something special in it?"

"Yes, there was. The director of postal services has had a heart attack and died. I have just given the order to begin printing the New Testaments."

It was legally possible to do so since the order to confiscate Bibles had been rescinded in response to my letter to the government leaders. In my letter, let us not forget, I had written, "you might even be found 'to fight against God!'" (Acts 5:39)

God Himself ensures that His good will in this world is carried out. He clears the way, gently if possible and if not...

These events represent only a handful of the milestones in the pioneering phase of this work of Bible distribution.

Chapter 14

New Printing Arrangements

The *Evangeliipress*

The demand for Bibles continued. Dr. Myron Sackett had been faithful in securing from America the funds needed for publication costs. In August 1967 he suddenly passed away. This meant the end of this source of financial assistance.

I wrote to Hallzon in Sweden and asked whether the late Dr. Sackett had taken care of all the bills for our Bibles and whether it was yet possible to place more orders. I also asked him if he felt that there was any chance of relying on the support of Oral Roberts who had provided the late Dr. Sackett with an office in his Tulsa, Oklahoma headquarters. It seemed to me that they had worked together to some extent, in the supplying of funds for Bibles.

Hallzon replied that Roberts would not become involved whatsoever, as his focus of interest was the university founded in his name.

I wrote him another letter saying I believed that my Lord would give me all the funds needed for printing costs and in faith I ordered an additional ten thousand copies of the Hebrew Bible. From that time on we have arranged for the printing of Hebrew Bibles on our own. The Lord has been faithful and has taken care of the costs. Three hundred thousand copies have been printed and distributed in Israel.[1]

Later, I requested a license for importing this above-mentioned shipment; in spite of our previous experiences. Over the course of the first twenty years of our ministry we actually received such a license only twice. The rest of the shipments came through by other means.

The Hebrew Bible is of course a virtual need in this country, most of all since it is a public school textbook! Due to the influx of new immigrants from non-Hebrew-speaking countries, the need for Bibles in many other languages has greatly increased. Particularly the older generation of immigrants is particularly grateful for a Bible in their own language. So our ministry expanded to reach "the ends of the earth" that suddenly appeared at "our doorstep" as it were. We have printed the Bible in over fifteen languages.

Hundreds of thousands of immigrants have arrived from Romania since Israel became a state. We put out a search warrant for any copies of the Bible in Romanian but it turned out that only a minimal number of them were available anywhere. I made a trip to Finland, contacted the University of Helsinki librarian and told her that I absolutely had to get a hold of a Romanian New Testament that included the Psalms. She was not at all sure that such a book existed in their library but she promised to look into the matter. It was indeed found! I explained for which purpose I need the book and received it on loan.

The Evangeliipress made two successive editions of it. The first twenty thousand were distributed in no time so we had another fifteen thousand printed in 1962. To the best of my knowledge, our printing of the Romanian Scriptures was the only printing of its kind in the past several decades. Large numbers were happily received not only in Israel but also by various organizations in England as well as by contacts in Vienna who took care of getting them into Romania.

We have also printed Russian Bibles for the immigrants from the former Soviet Union. Already by 1978 we ordered the first printing of thirty-five thousand copies. The Russian/Hebrew New Testaments we receive from London are especially desired by the new immigrants.

---

[1] This figure is valid to the end of 1978.

God's Word for the Arabs

Until 1967, we distributed God's Word only to the Jews -Hebrew Bibles to schools, *kibbutzes*, and to Hebrew-language classes for new immigrants. In March 1967, the Lord told me, "You must now start getting Arabic New Testaments." I began by calling the Bible Society and asked them how many Arabic New Testaments they could sell me. The answer was, "A couple of hundred at most." I felt that would not be enough to get started so I wrote to our press in Sweden and asked for twenty thousand copies to be ready by June 15. They agreed to my request.

That summer, I was on a visit to Finland, at the Kauniainen Bible School's annual Israel festival. Conveniently, Hallzon of the Evangeliipress was there and provided me with sample copies my order. We settled the payment and agreed on shipping the lot immediately in my name, to the port at Haifa.

In the 1973 Six-Day War, over a million Arabs found themselves in Israeli territory. A month after the war we were able to begin distributing God's word to them. In Muslim countries, it is illegal to distribute God's Word. Israel is not in this category.

Some time later, three brothers involved in ministry to the Arabs came to us: a school principal, an indigenous pastor from Nazareth and an American Christian worker. They confirmed the fact that there was a great need for Bibles among their people. I told them that I had printed and distributed Arabic New Testaments.

"We are certainly grateful for those you have distributed." They came to express however, that the religious Muslims specifically want the entire Bible. "Why?" I asked. "Is it not enough to provide them with the New Testament which clearly presents the way of salvation?"

They explained that that the Old Testament contains the story of Ishmael that relates the historical fact that Abraham is Ishmael's father whom God promised to make a great nation. In addition, they read with joy the curses declared by the prophets against the Jewish people. Now they have heard rumors that God has promised nevertheless to have mercy on the Jews, and to bring them back to this land which He promised them as their heritage and their homeland. They cannot believe these promises without reading them for themselves, from an Arabic Bible. These Muslims claim that we will never achieve peace between Jews and Arabs until they themselves can read about these promises and then believe that it is God Himself who has brought the Jews back to this land as He has promised in His Word.

I asked them why the Bible Society had not taken care of this matter. They said that the largest Christian publishing company in the Middle East was in Beirut. Since connections to Lebanon had been broken and because of the unrest, they had not been able to print God's Word any longer. I knew this to be the case, and that they themselves actually had no Bibles.

I suggested to the brothers that we go before the Lord and seek His will in this question. As we prayed, the Lord said, "This is the "new need" of which I have spoken to you about. Order five thousand Arabic Bibles now and use the special $1,500 gift as a down-payment for them."

"New need" was the expression used by a Finnish sister who had come to me about a month before this meeting about Arab Bibles. She had said, "You will soon have new needs in your work. The Lord told me to give this $1,500 for that purpose." I asked her what those "new needs" might be. "I don't know," she answered. "The Lord will surely let you know at the right time."

I told the brothers, "It is definitely God's will that the Arabs also receive Bibles in their own language. I will order 5,000 copies immediately. Just a moment while I fetch the money that we will give as a down payment for them." They gave me a receipt for the $1,500. Three months later, this first shipment of Arabic Bibles arrived. By 1987 we had a total of 60,000 copies printed.

On another occasion, the Lord encouraged me to print 40,000 copies of the Gospel of John in Arabic. The Evangeliipress was again of good service to us. When they arrived, I packed my car full and first took them to Jerusalem. I was there for two days, taking them to several distribution centers. Left with about a thousand copies, I asked the Lord for advice regarding what I should do with the remainder. I really didn't want to simply store them in the Tiberias warehouse.

The Lord said, "Take them quickly to V.S."

I protested, saying, "Don't you know that he is a Messianic believer who has his own printing press? Surely he doesn't need them!"

The Lord said, "Take them there quickly."

I obeyed and went to see V.S. I asked him whether he knew of anyone who needed the Gospel of John in Arabic. "I have about a thousand copies in my car," I said.

To my astonishment, he answered, "I was just visited by a certain Arab pastor who has been unsuccessfully searching for some for many months. He was here a while ago to inquire if I could print some for him. I told him I didn't have time to do so. He is presently in the yard trying to start his car. Go quickly to see if you can get a hold of him."

Running outside, I saw that he was just about to leave! I raised my hand and stood in front of his car. He rolled down the window, naturally wondering what was the problem. I asked him, "Are you the pastor who is searching for the Gospel of John in Arabic?"

He answered, "Yes, I have been searching for several months. Where can I get some?"

"From my car, right over here," I said, pointing to my vehicle.

He was very surprised, to say the least! He had prepared a correspondence course on that particular Gospel and there were about eight hundred students ready to begin their study if only they had what to study from!

A few days later, the next command from my Master was this: "Take three thousand copies of that Gospel in Arabic immediately to the Nazareth EMMS Hospital." I took them there the very same day. They were happy to receive them. A few days later I left to take some more to Haifa. I succeeded in finding suitable destinations for a large number of them but once again, by the end of the day, I had about a thousand copies left in my car. So as usual, I asked the Lord for advice.

His answer was simple and direct: "Nazareth EMMS Hospital."

"But Lord, only a few days ago they received a large quantity. Surely they won't need these now," I protested.

The command was clear: "Take them there!"

Upon arrival, I met B.W., the brother to whom I had given the three thousand copies earlier. I told him, "In the car I have a thousand copies of the Gospel left, but surely you don't need any more since you have already received so many not long ago."

"We don't have a single copy left. Thank the Lord that you brought more! Come have lunch with us. I will tell you more as we sit down," answered the brother.

During our meal he told me a story of which I had already read in the newspapers. In Samaria there is an Arab city by the name of Jenin. In a certain home late at night, peculiar things began to happen. Unseen beings began to move about in the house and dreadful voices could be heard throughout the night. The people were very frightened and couldn't sleep at night. A Muslim priest had been brought in, to calm the "ghosts." He had pasted pages from the Koran on the walls but that had not helped. The entire city was tense and frightened. I had read about it in the Jerusalem Post.

In a state of hopelessness, they got in touch with two Christian Arab pastors and asked for their help. The pastors prayed and fasted and then went to the home. Noticing the pages of the Koran pasted on the walls, they requested that these be torn down at once and destroyed. After general questioning, they asked what had been done last of all in the house before the ghosts began to act. Finally they found out that the family had held spiritualist séances late at night. The pastors realized that this was the real reason for these apparitions, and they explained it to the frightened family.

The Bible strongly forbids any contact with the spirits of darkness. If one calls them to himself, it is difficult to get rid of them. And there is only One, Yeshua, the Son of God, who can bring freedom and release from their power.

The ghosts were exorcised after the family promised to repent of their activities. They wanted to know more about this Yeshua who has the power to free people from the control of the powers and principalities of darkness. The pastors explained that they didn't have with them the kind of literature that they needed, in Arabic, but that the Nazareth EMMS Hospital could provide them with it. And so a couple of men from Jenin traveled to the hospital for the literature about Yeshua! They were the ones that received the three thousand copies of the Gospel of John that I had taken there on the previous day. There was a revival in Jenin, and several other families were converted. Later on, they requested also Arabic Bibles and more New Testaments.

The Arab Christian leaders requested bilingual Gospels in Arabic and English. I didn't know of anyone who had published such an edition. So I decided to have the Gospel of Luke translated. Our friend Heikki Palva, Professor of Arabic at the University of Helsinki, carefully edited the final version. For the cover we chose a color photo of the Dome of the Rock in the Old City of Jerusalem, cherished by the Arabs. When they receive it, they even kiss the picture on the cover.

The first printing of 25,000 copies was immediately distributed. The second order of 25,000 was made soon after, and it too was gone quickly! Many from the third printing of 30,000 copies were sent straight to the USA (for the Ford factories that have numerous Arab-speaking employees) as well as to several Arab countries.

There are approximately 1,200 million Muslims in the world. The world's 160 million Arabs are almost all Muslim. They firmly believe that every Arab has to be a Muslim. Arab Christians are hated and persecuted. In Lebanon there used to be quite a large Christian population, but for some time now, there have been terrible persecutions against them. During the PLO-regime, tens of thousands of Lebanese Christians were killed. Even today life is not easy for them. Israel is perhaps the only nation that has supported them. We have sent the Word of God in Arabic to Lebanon as well. When the archbishop of Lebanon was on a visit to Israel, he came to visit us personally to thank us for our gifts.

Islam is a world of darkness, proud in spirit, which keeps hundreds of millions of people in slavery. The Word of God is the best antidote against this. Only the Prince of Peace, Yeshua the Son of God, will be able to establish peace between the descendants of Ishmael and Isaac.

Chapter 15

God's Wisdom and Timing

Over-Sized Crates

The work of distributing Bibles is not as simple a task as some would be inclined to think. There are often problems to attend to that come upon us unannounced. The issue of the import license has been only one of many complications.

On a particular occasion, nine tons of Hebrew and Arabic New Testaments were on their way. I had warned the shippers beforehand that they should not pack the books into crates that are too large. Since we have no crane for lifting heavy articles, everything has to be done by manpower only.

It was the rainy season, on a morning in March that I received a phone call. At the other end of the line there was a truck driver who said, "I have brought your Bible shipment. Hurry to unload it because I don't even have a tarp with me and it could start to rain."

I called Kalervo, our son, and asked him to come help quickly. We went together to the Scottish Mission where the huge vehicle was parked. It had nine wooden crates, each weighing over a ton, each one as large as a child's playhouse. Seeing them, I was overwhelmed. So I sighed, *Oh,*

God's Wisdom and Timing

dear Heavenly Father! What should we do now that our Bibles are in such an inconvenient spot on the side of the highway, right where the road is so narrow? We couldn't even imagine beginning to unload there. Those crates were like tank barricades that would close all traffic to the north. And how could we lower them? Even ten men couldn't lift one crate out of the truck, they would destroy themselves trying to do so. *Lord, be merciful and give us wisdom! These are not my books, they are Yours! Tell us what we should do in order to get this shipment unloaded before we get caught in the rain*!

Immediately, the Lord began to instruct me. "The Scots have a courtyard. Send Kalervo to measure the width of the courtyard gate and drive the truck in there!"

So I sent Kalervo with a rope to measure the width of the gate. We discovered that there was an inch to spare on either side of the truck if it were to enter through the opening into the courtyard. I showed the measurements to the driver and told him, "If you have passed your driver's test, you should be able to drive through that." He stared at me and then said, "I'll give it a try!"

Slowly, slowly, the truck growled its way in low gear into the courtyard. The next step was to get the crates down from the truck without a hoisting device.

Lord, advise us on how to proceed, please! I prayed. At that moment I saw, as if on a movie film, three iron pipes. I had never seen crowbars in Israel. But at that moment, the idea flashed in my mind. I ran to the closest hardware store and asked for four iron pipes, an inch in diameter and two meters in length. These we then used as we would a crowbar! We were able to get the bottom of a crate raised enough to put a pipe under it, like a castor wheel. The truck was then driven up a slight incline in the yard and I noticed that another pipe was also useful to slide under the crate. By exploiting the law of gravity, we were able to get the crates off the truck -one by one to its own corner of the yard. Soon, the courtyard was nearly full of Bible crates.

The director of the Scottish Mission was upset. "Our vehicle can't get out to go anywhere since you've blocked the road on all sides," he complained angrily.

"Give me a few hours to clear up the congestion," I assured him.

Now we needed helpers, quick. I went to the Hartman Hotel where the Finnish tourists usually like to stay. It turned out that one group had a day off just then. I explained the situation to the group leader and that we were in need of help, in a hurry!

"It's good that at times we can even get in a little work as part of our tour!" He said, calling his people together.

About ten of them came with me, and we set up an assembly line of sorts to dissemble the crates! Together we opened them with claw hammers. Fortunately, the contents were in packages of ten boxes each. Kalervo and I packed the small automobile time and again, and drove back and forth between the warehouse and the courtyard. Before the rain began, we had finished. One crate was left intact to serve as a playhouse for Kalervo's children. It rained hard that night.

The next time, I ordered a shipment weighing five tons, but I implored them never again to send them in such large crates!

A Strike at the Harbor

Another time, we had a struggle with a shipment from London. Six to seven thousand Hebrew/Russian New Testaments were coming as a gift from London. I had succeeded in acquiring an import permit, to be used within an allotted time period.

I was expecting the books to arrive any day. Then came the notice from London with an announcement: *There is a strike at the harbor here and it looks as if it will not end. What should we do since the import permit is in danger of becoming invalid?*

"There are other harbors in England. Send them by way of Hull," I replied. "They are not striking there."

The books were indeed sent to Hull, but the devil got there before they did! As the strike ended in London, another one began in Hull! Now we were in real trouble. With a friend, I began to pray, *Dear Father in Heaven! Make the devil's attempts come to naught! End that strike at Hull to enable Your books to come through*!

One day before the import permit was to expire, the strike at Hull ended; the papers were officially stamped on the last day possible day. We were safe since the permit was dependent on the departure date of the shipment, not on its arrival in the land.

God's Wisdom and Timing

Excavations

The strike was not the last of the devil's pitfalls in regard to this shipment.

Our warehouse is right next to a highway. At that time, the municipality began digging an extensive sewer system along the side of the road. They began the ditch digging at a distance from our warehouse but definitely in our direction. It was like a giant snake, a meter wide and a meter and a half deep. The excavated dirt was moved to the other side of the highway.

Distressed, I began to pray, *Dear Heavenly Father! If that excavation reaches us now, we won't be able to get the Bible shipment into the warehouse. The whole road will be blocked!*

On top of it all, I was due to leave on vacation to Finland. I called the shipping agent and said, "Try to get the goods out of the harbor as quickly as possible. Take a special vehicle and let those wheels roll fast! We must hurry in order to get the Bibles to the warehouse ahead of the ditch diggers."

The Lord answered my prayer above and beyond my expectations: An air drill was being used to loosen the earth. The drill broke, and for three days the excavation stopped. During those three days we were able to load all of the Bibles into the warehouse!

When I returned from Finland, I went to inspect the excavations. In front of the warehouse there was now a pile of dirt, mud and stones. It was a hard job to get the entrance area cleared up, in order to get into the warehouse. But my heart was full of thanks to the Lord for His perfect timing!

Traveling Mercies in North America

In the beginning of the 1980s, I went on a tour of Canada and the United States, via Finland. I had met a Messianic believer from North Carolina who sent me the funds for the trip and asked me to visit him.

Since I belonged to *Suomi Seura* (The Finland Society), I took their charter flight to Vancouver. There I took part in the North American Finns' Summer Festival. My next stop was to be North Carolina. The night before my flight, I stopped at a ticket agency to confirm my reservation. I then wired my host to let him know the flight details so he could come and meet me.

Upon arrival in Seattle for a stop-over, one of the ground attendants warned me: "There's a strike here and there is time for only one plane to depart for the South and it is completely booked."

"Oh no," I said in anguish. "I have to inform the gentleman meeting me that I cannot make the plane that I have promised to be on." So I began to search for a telegraph office. Surprisingly, I couldn't find one anywhere at that airport.

I wanted to buy a map of the United States, so that I could plan my trip. The airport had all sorts of kiosks and shops but no American maps! Finally, I was rather hungry so I sat down for a bowl of soup.

Then I took the "route" most familiar to me. I prayed, *Dear Heavenly Father! The devil is at his game again. In no way would he want me to see that believing brother of mine. Now help me quickly, and tell me what I should do!*

A distinguished looking gentleman was walking in the hallway. I heard the familiar inner voice which said, *Go to that gentleman and tell him about your problem!*

I went to him and said, "This is a strange airport. I can't seem to find a telegraph office anywhere!"

"Indeed there was one here once but no longer," he replied.

"Well, how do people take care of their affairs?" I asked.

"There's an office here called the 'Traveler's Aid' and they will call wherever you wish if you provide them with the telephone number."

Realizing the man's resourcefulness, I continued: "I am a Finnish Christian working in Israel. I would have bought a map of the United States but unfortunately they don't seem to sell them here in the airport. Now it's essential that I get a flight to North Carolina, my trip back to Vancouver will automatically be cancelled if I cannot depart from here immediately."

He listened patiently and then said, "Come into my office for a moment!"

I soon noticed that he was one of the airport's highest-ranking officials. He called several numbers and finally said, "We do indeed have a rather difficult situation here, but from Gate 16 the last available plane will be leaving in a couple of hours. You can continue your journey. I will give you the last available seat. Here is your ticket! Call from the 'Traveler's Aid' office to tell your friend when you are arriving. You won't be delayed by much."

And so it was. When I boarded the plane, I was placed in tourist class, which I had naturally anticipated. But the flight attendant came to me and said, "No, no, sir! You have a first-class ticket." She took me to the separate section and served me first when the time came for a meal.

I had received the seat of a VIP, the only one vacant on that plane.

During that trip to America, I stopped in Chicago, to visit our daughter Mirja's in-laws. They had been Christian workers in China for several years. From there I was to travel via Seattle to Vancouver, and then back to Finland. At the Chicago airport, as I asked to reserve a seat on the flight from Seattle, I was told, "We can't guarantee a seat for you. A strike is beginning tonight and planes won't be flying until the strike is over."

I left on my trip anyway, in faith. I prayed, *Dear Heavenly Father! The plane is leaving tomorrow from Vancouver to Finland and if I don't get there in time, I'll have to pay a return fare again. Help me in Your mercy so that I can get on that last plane.*

With my heart pumping, I hurried to the Seattle airport and heard that the last plane was about to depart for Vancouver. The line of passengers was beginning to board the plane. The check-in agent wondered why I didn't have my seat reserved, but then he said, "There is one vacant seat left. You may have that." Once again, I had good reason to thank the Lord.

A Quick Meeting

On my last visit to Finland, I had to see the director of the Evangeliipress. Hallzon was a busy man. He didn't have the time then to come to Finland nor did I have the time to go to Sweden. He suggested that he travel from Orebro to Stockholm on a given Monday, when he had to take care of other business in the capital anyway, and I fly from Helsinki to the Arland airport to meet him at 9:00 A.M. Thus we would have one hour to discuss printing issues. Our plan was indeed successful and we were able to take care of business.

That same evening I was to speak at the Vilppula *Evangelista* Home, at 5:00 P.M. To get there on time, I had made a reservation on a rapid transit train leaving from Helsinki at 2:00 P.M. Maire was already there, together with many of our friends from various places.

The flight was scheduled to arrive at the Helsinki airport at 1:15 P.M. That left me with forty-five minutes before the train was to leave. *I have plenty of time*, or so I thought.

The departure from Sweden was delayed. We were waiting for some important person, and he seemed to be quite late. Worrying, I wondered how the evening's meeting would work out.

At last, the person we were waiting for came, and we were able to take off. We arrived in Helsinki at 1:35 P.M. It was very late. I again turned with earnest to the Father, praying that He would allow a miracle to take place so that I might reach the train in time.

A large group of travelers was waiting for a taxi. There were none to be seen a mile away. I said to the ones who were at the head of the line-up: "I am a Finn living in a foreign country and I am only visiting here. I must get to the Helsinki train station to catch a rapid transit train that leaves at 2:00 P.M." Those at the head of the line nodded their assent to my request. "Go first!" they said.

Immediately a taxi appeared. I hopped in and said, "To the Helsinki train station just as fast as you can!"

It happened so conveniently that on the same plane was a visitor whom the Finnish government officials had come to meet, obviously the same man who had delayed the departure of our plane. From around the corner, a diplomatic limousine, equipped with bodyguards, whizzed out and "paved the way" to Helsinki. My taxi joined the procession and we drove fast. The traffic lights had been disconnected, and so we arrived at the station at the appointed time. Five minutes before 2:00 P.M., I was sitting in the train, wondering whether it was true or if it was a dream. To get to the Helsinki train station from the airport in a matter of twenty minutes was certainly a miracle of God.

Chapter 16

Gleanings

The Children's Home Director

In distributing God's Word among the Israelis, we often find ourselves meeting the most different kinds of people. During the time we lived in Dr. Heart's holiday home, a director of a children's home came regularly to visit us. For over a year she kept coming back to see us and we extended our hospitality and friendship to her. During that time, we prayed a great deal on her behalf, but in no way did we pressure her to make a decision to become a believer in Yeshua. The petals of a rosebud cannot be opened by force. The rose will open naturally as the sun shines on it.

One day she came by taxi to tell us something very important.

"What is it that is so important?" we queried.

"I have been coming to visit you now and then for well over a year and I am completely convinced that Yeshua is the Son of God and the Messiah. Now I want to be baptized."

"Do you understand that this is a very serious step? You will be persecuted by your own people," I warned.

"Yes, I know but first I have one crucial question. If you baptize me, do I have to join the Lutheran Church of Finland?"

"Most definitely not! I am not here as a representative of any church denomination. I am here as a representative of Yeshua, the Son of God. You, a Messianic believer, can decide your denominational views according to the teachings of the New Testament. Baptism is done in the name of the Father, Son and the Holy Spirit, not in the name of any church."

She seemed pleased and said, "Had I known this, I would have long ago asked to be baptized. I visited an English Christian organization in Jerusalem and asked them the same question but the pastor replied that of course I would be joining their church if I were to be baptized by them. I would be very happy if you would baptize me."

So we went ahead and held a small baptismal ceremony at sunrise on the shore of the Sea of Galilee. I baptized her in the Messiah's "favorite" lake, in front of our house. She was a blissfully happy woman as the taxi took her back to her home, to the shelter for handicapped children.

L.W., who had been present at the baptism, left on vacation to Switzerland, her homeland. While she was there, she told people that also in Israel, people became believers and she mentioned having been a witness to the baptism of a director of a children's home in the Sea of Galilee. Unfortunately, she mentioned the name of this woman.

As a result, some time later, a government inspector came to see her at the home, holding a German newspaper. In large print, the headline read, "Damned missionaries have baptized a director of a children's home. How can the government give aid to this kind of home with a Christian director?"

"Is it true what is written here?" he inquired.

"It is true to the extent that I have been baptized."

"In which church has your name been registered?"

"I firmly believe that my name has been written in the Book of Life in heaven."

"Who is that congregation's head?"

"It is Yeshua, our Messiah. He is the head of the congregation."

"Who baptized you?" he demanded to know.

"That is entirely a personal matter. I will not tell you." She was wise not to say!

"As you well understand, we can no longer consider this an official children's home," the inspector said. "Because you have become a Christian, government aid can no longer be granted for this endeavor. The children will be taken away at once, and the home will be closed."

And so it was. The director accepted the situation calmly and left her future in God's hands. She had worked hard, so a brief "job-search vacation" was very welcome.

A Fresh Start

A week or two passed as she pondered what to do, when one evening someone knocked at her door, and a voice asked somewhat guardedly, "Is this the children's home whose director is a Christian? Are you that person?"

When she said yes, the visitor became bolder and started to explain. "We have a handicapped child and I have been looking for a good Christian shelter which would take him in. Would you take him here? I am ready to pay whatever you require."

"Well there is plenty of room in the house at present. Bring him here."

It was not long before the home was again full of children brought by various individuals. And once again, there was even a waiting list for new residents.

This is a concrete example of how "the Lord in His mercy cares for His own in Zion," as we sing in a beautiful hymn with these words.

Once I stopped in at the home to see how they were getting along. With me were several Finnish tourists. One of the children, already six or seven years old, was not able to walk but crawled along the floor.

"Take a picture of this child!" the director urged.

Since I had a camera with me, I took a snapshot of her.

She asked that we pray on her behalf so that she could one day be able to walk. We prayed together right then and there, leaving the matter with the Lord.

It was at least a year after this visit before I found my way to the home again. When she saw it was me, the director called for one of the children to come say hello.

A small, perky little girl came to me, curtsied nicely and looked at me with smiling eyes.

"Do you remember this girl?" the director asked.

"No, I'm sure that I've never seen her before," I had to admit.

"What? You haven't seen her even though you took a picture of her!?"

"A picture? Me? Definitely not!"

"This is the same girl who crawled along the floor, on whose behalf we prayed a year ago. She is well now. The Lord strengthened her legs and now she plays and runs just as well as the others."

The Rabbi's Son

A rabbi came to the home and told of his great sorrow: "I have a son who has a tumor in his brain, and because of it he has severe, persistent headaches. The doctors are ready to operate but they say that the chances of a successful operation are very slim. They can't guarantee the results because the operation could cause brain damage. I have to decide whether or not to go ahead with it."

"Could you take care of the boy here? I will pay whatever you want," the desolate father pleaded.

On this occasion, I happened to be there, together with a visitor from overseas. As we spoke with the director, she mentioned the rabbi's son. She asked if we could pray for him so that God would perform the operation of which the doctors were so unsure.

And so before we left, the boy came to us and we prayed, asking God to heal him.

A long time passed before I visited the home again. This time, I remembered the boy and asked first of all how the boy with the headaches was feeling.

"The boy is fine!" the director told us. "A doctor comes here once a month to examine the health of the children. On one of these visits, he noticed an unusual lump on the boy's neck. "Thank God!" he had exclaimed. "Now the growth which has pressed against the child's brain is being naturally discharged through his neck."

And so it happened. One day there was no trace left of the lump. The headaches were gone, and the boy was well.

I noticed several kinds of chocolate boxes scattered here and there, both full ones and empty ones! "You have really splurged," I said, laughing. "Chocolate is awfully expensive in this country, isn't it?"

"I didn't buy them!" she said. "The rabbi whose son experienced the healing has brought them to us. You can imagine his gratefulness about what happened to his son."

The Bookshop Owner

Friends called from Haifa about a retired bookshop owner who had broken her leg and who had to get to Tiberias to bathe in the hot springs. "This lady is in deep need of spiritual guidance," they said. "Since you live so close to the springs, could you put her up for a while?"

We were somewhat uncertain at first, about how we would be able to help such a refined lady and to serve as her hosts but the person calling assured us that this visitor was a very undemanding person. The main idea was to provide her with "spiritual help."

We agreed. My first question to her was to inquire which language she was comfortable with.

"I know Russian best," she answered. "I immigrated some years ago. I do know English as well, and Hebrew of course."

It is our custom to always read from God's Word and to pray for a while after breakfast, a custom that we did not neglect during her stay.

We have recordings of the Gospels in several languages. I took them out and gave her the Russian ones to listen to. The lady played the Gospel records throughout the day. "You can't imagine what fine records you have!" she would declare with satisfaction.

Within the month that she stayed in our home she came to believe in the Messiah and made a clear decision, without reservations, on her own initiative, to be a follower of our Lord.

We corresponded for a while but then she broke contact. I had a very strong urge to go without delay to see how she was doing. Her address was in Tel Aviv so I traveled there immediately. She was not at home but someone who knew her told me that her foot had started to trouble her again and that she had been taken to hospital.

It was not visiting hours when I arrived at the hospital. "I have traveled all the way from Tiberias, since this morning, in order to see her," I explained. "Couldn't you permit me to see her for even fifteen minutes, just to greet her? I know for certain that she would be glad to see me because she is our friend."

They gave me permission. She was very pale and appeared to be in weak condition but on seeing me she had no trouble expressing her joy! "The best time in my life was when I was at your home in Tiberias," she said. "It was there that I came to know my Saviour. It was as if everywhere around there He was so close to me...."

After we had talked for a while, we prayed, and I left her in the Lord's care. Fifteen minutes go by so quickly. I assured her that God isn't restricted to a certain time or place. He is just as real everywhere, even in a hospital. So much depends on our own attitude and the condition of our heart.

I felt somewhat embarrassed because I had visited a patient in hospital and hadn't even brought flowers. So I wrote a letter to her brother, asking him to buy a bouquet on our behalf the next time he went to visit his sister. I enclosed a little money for it. I had been in such a hurry that the flowers had simply slipped my mind.

A few days later I received a letter from her brother with the money I had sent, returned in the envelope. His note read: "My dear sister doesn't need anything any longer. The night after you had been to see her, she passed away."

We believe that she was one of those who has been "reaped" from the "field" of this world into the storehouse of God's Kingdom in Heaven.

A Psychiatrist

Friends in Jerusalem called me and told me about a psychiatrist who was in a depression. He was currently on vacation and planned to spend time at the hot springs. They asked if I could you possibly take him for the ten days that he was to be in Tiberias, "since above all else, he is in need of spiritual help?"

Honestly speaking, we were not particularly interested in taking this man into our home because of the hardly encouraging advance information we received about him. But since our friends felt this to be so important and because they promised to pray for us daily, we finally agreed.

When the doctor arrived we couldn't help but notice certain things. His fingers were stained yellow from nicotine; a sign of a heavy smoker. We were not mistaken. In fact, the constant smell of cigarette fumes was truly bothersome. Immediately after every meal he had to "light up."

Yet we had promised to put up with him for ten days. Every now and then we sighed to the Lord, asking Him to help us deal with his habit. We of course did not express our discomfort nor did he ask our permission to smoke.

Several days passed. We were as usual, sitting together and he was puffing away. I sat there asking the Lord how long we would need to deal with this stench. Suddenly the man said, "I am such a poor wretch, a slave to nicotine as you can see. And this is not the only bad habit that I have. Do you believe that one can be freed of this addiction?"

"Yes, one can." I replied.

"How can you be so sure?" he asked.

"From my own experience," I responded. "I smoked for ten years before I became a believer. I even smoked cigars and I was a slave to nicotine in the same way that you are today. People would tell me that it is almost impossible to be freed from it. But when I gave my entire life to Yeshua and trusted in the merit of His bloodshed as payment for the sins of all mankind, including my own, He freed me from this addiction and from everything else that I needed to be freed of. Surrendering completely to God is the condition by which one can be free."

We talked a long time and I assured him that this was the only way to freedom, inner peace and rest. "Yeshua frees everyone who comes to him, and the shackles of sin are broken. 'Minor repairs' do not help when you are seeking a real change in your life."

We talked some more. Finally he said, "Could you pray that I too can be free of tobacco and that God would renew me completely?"

So we knelt then and there. I placed my hand firmly on his head and pleaded, *Dear Heavenly Father, in the blessed name of Yeshua, cast out from this man those demons of nicotine and every other addiction and cleanse him by faith in Yeshua's blood and receive him as your child! Yeshua, You yourself have promised that whosoever comes to You, You will not cast out. Here is a person who has come to You and who needs You.*

At the end, I said to him, "Now you pray yourself, in your own words so that the Lord will know that you really mean it."

In a very childlike and simple way, he then asked that the Lord would accept him and free him from all his ties with sin that had bound him.

The Lord hears and he helps us. To this day, from that moment on, his situation changed. He was freed from tobacco. He wanted to know everything possible about the new life living as a believer, studying the Bible. We spoke about baptism and he wanted to take this step as well.

The man related to me a few of the milestones on his personal "road to salvation." He told of his upbringing in a secular Jewish family in Hungary. They would celebrate the traditional holidays -the New Year, Day of Atonement, Passover- but he was never familiarized with the Old Testament writings of the prophets, much less the New Testament.

He related his story like this:

> In 1946, I met a Hungarian girl who was especially pleasant and appealing to me. I didn't understand at the time that this was the result of her living faith in Yeshua. I enjoyed being with her and we were friends until one day something completely unexpected happened. The girl began to tell me of the return of the Jews to the Lord. She showed me chapter seven of the Book of Revelation where it speaks of Israel and those who will be called "God's servants." She was the first person to ever speak to me about the salvation of Israel and of our future task. My worldly mind could not handle this! It made me very angry and I immediately broke our relationship.
>
> Ten years later, when I had already moved to Israel, I felt a remarkable urge to study the Old Testament, particularly the prophets. The Book of Isaiah especially moved me but it took about eight years before I began to understand it and the other prophets correctly. From Daniel 9:26 I discovered that the Messiah would be cut off because of my sins and the sins of my nation Israel: *After threescore and two weeks shall Messiah be cut off, but not for himself: and the people of the prince that shall come shall destroy the city and the sanctuary; and the end thereof shall be with a flood, and unto the end of the war desolations are determined.*
>
> Then in 1962 I came into contact with the New Testament and consequently came to know Yeshua as the Saviour and Messiah. As a doctor, the fact of the resurrection was an obstacle for me because it

could not be logically explained. This was cause enough to postpone baptism and a final decision. My believing friends were a great help in these struggles, as well as my wife who had been a believer since her youth. My struggle became a crisis and drove me to the brink of despair. One night, my wife took matters "into her own hands" and said, "You are a doctor but I have a prescription for you!" We knelt beside the bed and asked the Lord to remove all doubts in Yeshua's name. A miracle happened and I was freed from the oppressive doubts. Consequently I was baptized in the Jordan River.

It was on this occasion that he was in our home and we partook for the first time in the Communion together, the meal in remembrance of the Lord's death and suffering.

Our guest returned to his home and his job a new man.

His colleagues immediately noticed a change in him. For one, tobacco no longer suited him. The rumor began to spread, "The doctor has become a Christian!"

He describes the series of incidents following his conversion, which led to his being refused the promotion that had been promised to him in his job. His trial period of one year at the hospital had come to an end and he was to receive permanence. Having blamelessly carried out his duties, there was no professional reason for the denial.

The doctor explained why:

In 1965 about twenty young Jews became believers in the coastal city of Ashdod. When this became known, persecution began against them. The local yeshiva students reacted with violence, threatening and attacking them even in their homes. Due to the dangerous situation, two of the young girls came to Jerusalem, to seek refuge with my wife. I myself was abroad at the time. Nevertheless, my name appeared in the newspaper and it was also reported that a Jewish doctor's wife had kidnapped two young girls from their parents in order to convert them to Christianity. This kind of news of course came to the attention of my superiors. I was henceforth treated as a traitor to my country because I had chosen to believe in Yeshua as the Messiah. Despite numerous attempts on my part to obtain a hearing with the minister of health, it was refused. I felt that I no longer had a place in my own nation. For this reason we emigrated from Israel.

I heard the full explanation only some years later, as he and his wife returned from their "exile" in England. At the time of their departure he hadn't informed us of the sad events, we heard of them from other sources. It is quite understandable that he took such great offense at this treatment, and left the country. Often Messianic believers experience this kind of misunderstanding and pressure from their own people. They need encouragement and our intercessory prayers.

When we heard that he had gone to London, we began to pray. *Dear Father in Heaven, take hold of our brother and bring him back in one way or another to Israel!*

He returned three years later, during the summer of 1967, when the Six-Day War broke out. This time, his offer of help to his country was more than welcome. He describes his sentiments while in London, having learned of the situation in Israel:

> My nation and my people were in peril. My wife and I wanted to return to Israel at once. I called the Israeli Embassy and volunteered my services. We had seats reserved on the next flight to Tel Aviv, and so we returned to Israel on the second day of the war in 1967.
>
> There was a great deal to be done. I tried my best to help my fellow countrymen and my superiors recognized my efforts. I was soon promoted in rank. Gradually the work became more and more burdensome and I gained weight so that I no longer had the strength to function as I had when I was younger. I began considering a changing to a job in a more peaceful environment.

The doctor called me for advice. I told him that I didn't think it was the Lord's intention to keep him in that same position for the rest of his life. "He surely has something else for you to do," I said.

"Good," he agreed. "I'll take your advice."

Later, he explained that a psychiatrist's job in this sector of society was under no circumstances a pleasant one. There were many complicated cases to deal with. In Israel, military service is three and a half years for men and close to two years for women. From time to time, some recruits pretend to be mentally ill. The psychiatrist's job is to determine whether the insane candidate is really insane or not. These cases can obviously be challenging.

An individual who has been exempted from service on grounds of insanity encounters serious dilemmas in civil life. He is also "exempt" from the right to drive. Potential employers naturally ask about the circumstances related to his military discharge and most are hesitant to hire the mentally ill. Consequently, such a person often returns to the doctor who examined him and admits to the lie. When the doctor discovers his mistake, he often feels disgusted, not to speak of discouraged.

It is no wonder that the doctor was greatly relieved when he resigned from his position.

But before he made a final decision on the issue, his wife visited our home in Tiberias. I happened to notice an advertisement for an available psychiatrist's position at a hospital that was soon to be opened. The doctor considered this to be a sign of God's direction and he applied. He was accepted!

However this new development was not the end of his difficulties. Soon after resigning from his position with the government, a slanderous article about him appeared in the newspaper. He was even accused of being a foreign spy! An extract from the article reads:

> How is it possible that there is in Israel's federal service, in an important position, a Christian man who has connections with missionaries? Who knows, he may be a foreign spy. This kind of individual should be immediately removed from government service.

It was truly God's mercy that the doctor had resigned just before the article appeared. As a result, the doctor would have faced further difficulties in his job. He naturally feared for the future, whether or not he would be accepted at a different workplace.

His fears proved to be unnecessary. The doctor was warmly received in his new position and he continues to be highly respected by his superiors as well as his patients.

He and his wife belong to a small group of believers in Yeshua. They can be compared to the first of the crop in the recently blossomed "fig tree" of Israel. We are now living in those times of which Yeshua spoke in the Gospel of Luke (22:29-31).

Another "Fig"

We had a dear friend, a young Jewish student in a Haifa technical school. He visited us often, and we spoke much about the Messiah of Israel. I gave him a Hebrew New Testament, which he studied carefully. One day he phoned me and told me that he believed Yeshua to be the Messiah. "I believe in Him and I want to be baptized," he confessed to me. I warned him of the troubles he was sure to encounter as a result.

"I know," he said, "but I am ready." He came to us and I baptized him in the Jordan River. In the next letter he told me, "My mother was crying, my father cursing and my brother threatened to kill me."

In Copenhagen there was to be a conference for Messianic believers and I helped him to go there. It was at this gathering that he found his wife, a lovely young Christian. He returned to Israel a married man. The couple lives in Haifa.

Chapter 17

Answers to Prayer

God Provides

The Davies of Philadelphia Pennsylvania have done a great work in spreading God's Word. They had the first 100,000 Hebrew New Testaments for Israel printed in the early part of this ministry. In March 1967, I received a letter from them. As I read it, I was overcome by a curious feeling, as if it was a farewell.

Mr. Davies had included a ten-dollar gift. He thanked me for our earlier joint cooperation. A small additional slip of paper in the envelope was a note from his wife: "My dear husband signed this letter at 6:00 P.M. and at 9:00 the Lord called him to his heavenly home. In two months time he would have been ninety-three years old. Until the end, he wrote letters by hand and was active in his duties."

Some time later, we needed more copies of the Gospel according to St. Matthew. I went to the press that had done the job earlier and inquired about the cost of printing 40,000 copies. I was told it would be 20,000 pounds, half a pound per copy. Two thousand pounds was required as a down payment, 10,000 in one month and the remainder to be paid upon delivery. I agreed to these terms.

I hadn't spoken to anyone about this need. One day, just as I was about to head off for the press to see how the order was progressing, a couple of tourists stopped by our home. Noticing that I was on my way out, they immediately told me that their business was to deliver an important letter from Finland.

"Maire is inside and she will serve you refreshments, please give the letter to her. I must leave now for Tel Aviv," I said and hurried to the car.

When I returned, I asked Maire if the guests had left a letter.

"Yes, they have!" she answered.

There was a large sum of money in the envelope, along with a short letter that read:

> The Lord told me to send this money for the printing of God's Word. My sister is coming to Israel on a trip and she will bring it to you. I am one of the emigrants from Karelia and I will by no means save money for the anti-Christ. We were already forced to leave our possessions once and that was enough.

A second gift that came later covered the rest of the cost of this printing. In the Keuruu parish of Finland there was a man of great faith. He had made a will which set aside 10,500 Finnish marks ($2,500 in 1987) for the printing of God's Word in Israel. He was in poor health, often in the hospital.

His wife had an idea. She told him, "Listen, dear husband. In a matter of days a group will be leaving for Israel. I have a feeling that we should withdraw the money now from the bank and sent it along with the group."

Their 10,500 marks paid the rest of the bill for the 40,000 copies of the Gospel. When I received the books, I sent a sample copy by special delivery to this couple in Keuruu, thanking them for the money. I explained in my letter that they had in a decisive way and at a very opportune time helped to pay for this printing.

I received a reply from his wife. "My dear husband received your special-delivery letter on the last day of his life. Together we thanked the Lord that the money we sent to you arrived on time and that the amount was so conveniently useful! Next time you visit Finland, come visit our home as well."

A Bad Accident

Our ever-conspiring opponent, the king of darkness, hates the Word of God. In every place he tries to prevent it from spreading. The devil knows that the Scripture is the best medicine against the disease of sin. In this country, especially, I have experienced the powerful opposition of the devil. Even my life has been at risk.

The first of three tries occurred on my trip to Bethlehem as I have described. The second was the near-explosion of three hand grenades in our yard. The third try was also a failure.

Our Bible warehouse was for a time in the lower part of Tiberias and our home on the outskirts of the city. Once when I was on the way home, driving as usual along one of the main roads in Tiberias. I had almost reached one of the major intersections, not having any intention to stop since I had the right of way. This time, I received a brisk order: "STOP right now. Put on the brakes!"

I recognized the Lord's voice.

I practically flew out the windshield because in city driving we don't tend to use seatbelts... For a second or two, I wondered why I had received such a command since the street in front of me was perfectly clear. I had just decided to continue on my way when I heard a tremendous crash. At first I didn't realize what had happened. It was like a bad dream. Pieces of cars and people were flying through the air. There was utter chaos on the street in front of me.

Suddenly a huge load of dirt landed with a bang on top of the whole mess. Shouting and moaning could be heard. What happened?

Four or five cars had been at the main intersection to my right, waiting their turn to drive through into the center of town. From behind, down the hill, came a twenty-five-ton truck full of dirt. Its brakes didn't hold and it drove right into the line of waiting cars, crushing them all. Five people were killed and fifteen hospitalized.

I had stopped ten meters from the scene. I had no intention of staying to watch as the ambulance came and to witness the desperate rescue efforts.

I drove home in solemnity but fervently thanking God for sparing me. This was the most serious automobile accident that had until then taken place in Tiberias. A sign has since been posted on the side of the road that forbids its use by heavy vehicles. They must circle the lake and enter Tiberias from the south.

A Rolling Boulder

Our home is at the foot of a big hill. One summer afternoon I was sitting outside, on the veranda of the kitchen, on a Finnish-made wooden chair. All of a sudden, the voice of the Lord said, "Get out of that chair right now! Go look at the orchard on the other side of the house!"

I obeyed and left my chair. I had hardly reached the other side of the house when I heard a loud crash. When I went back to see what had happened, I saw that the chair on which I had just been sitting had been crushed to pieces!

A shepherd boy on the top of the hill had loosened a large rock and it came like a rocket down the hill, crushing my chair and continuing on its way into the wall of our neighbor's house that was below us.

A stray dog had been lying next to the chair and in reaction to the crash he was in shock, running around the house whimpering. Maire heard the dog and came to ask me if I had been abusing the animal!

"I had no plans to harm anyone," I said, "but the devil was planning to kill me. But the Lord warned me just a bit before it was to happen." We used the wood of the chair for the sauna. Wood in Israel is scarce.

Chapter 18

God's Logic

Against all Odds

Long ago, when I resigned from my position as head of the railroad express office in Jyväskylä in order to answer God's calling to work in Israel, my decision caused a variety of reactions, misunderstandings for the most part.

For example, I wrote to my father and told him of my plan to spread the Word of God among the Jewish people. His answer to me was frank. Realizing that my future would henceforth be largely unpredictable, he wrote in reply:

> It is clear to me that you are a religious freak but to leave just now when you have reached a good position in your career, you decide to go overseas in search of adventure. You must be out of your mind. You should have your head examined and be put in care of a guardian. Your children should be taken from you so that you won't be able to take them with you to suffer want. How can they have any future over there?

The Lord in His mercy has cared for our whole family, in the most remarkable ways. It is true that Olavi did not receive more than a public school education in Finland and that Kalervo had to stop attending school in Sweden. When the family arrived in Israel, Mirja was so young that she was not yet of school age.

Olavi could have had the opportunity in Finland to prepare for whatever occupation he had wanted. Instead, he has studied on his own and owns a large library. The Lord led him to be the manager of the bookstore of the only Christian organization registered in southern Israel, in Beersheba. It is located in a newly built three-story building. Olavi has had all kinds of special experiences in his work.

Kalervo has driven the "Bible van" for many years, distributing God's Word to various parts of the country. He is a practical person and it seems nothing is beyond his expertise! He does all the repairs for us, both on the house and the car. He is a painter, electrician, first-class auto mechanic and in general a great help to us. We value his assistance even more now as Maire and I are getting older. Kalervo lives in the Tiberias vicinity. We are grateful that the Lord left us with at least one of the children close to us, working with us here "on site."

Rauha-Lilja and Mirja completed regular public school here in Israel. Rauha-Lilja went on to become a specialized nurse. She cares for the sick and the elderly in their homes, since 1975 in the Home Care Unit. She reports about her visits to the doctors, often dealing with unfortunate and unhappy people whose children have deserted them.

Mirja has concentrated on languages. When the Finnish Embassy requested me to refer them to someone who knew both the Finnish and Hebrew languages, I told them about my daughter who was at the time a student at the University of Helsinki. She would be a qualified person but I could not say on her behalf whether or not she would be interested in the job. The Finnish Foreign Minister got in touch with her and Mirja took a six-month special course for embassy secretaries. She was paid for taking the course. When the time came for her to begin work at the Finnish Embassy in Israel, she changed her mind. "Father, I wouldn't want to enter into this field at any price," she said. "To be a diplomat doesn't suit my character. I would much rather prefer to continue Hebrew studies at the Hebrew University."

So she continued her studies. The end result was not only an education but also a wedding! An American student asked her for Hebrew lessons and some time later they were engaged and married in the USA. They stayed there for a while and Mirja completed her BA in Humanities. Then they returned to Israel and Mirja went on to finish her MA in Hebrew, another in Clinical Psychology as well as a diplomas in Hebrew-English translation and Hebrew-language teaching.

Mirja's regular profession and field of expertise is psychology. She has worked as a psychologist in a hospital where she often met with unusual assignments. Once she was asked to determine which of the applicants for the study of medicine were to be accepted.

The Hebrew *Delitsch* translation of the New Testament is over one hundred years old. The Bible Society wanted a new translation in modern Hebrew so the translation committee began the search for experts. Our son-in-law, Mirja's husband was chosen as one of them, because of his knowledge of Greek. Mirja, as an expert in Modern Hebrew with a diploma in translation, was also chosen. It is actually quite remarkable that a Finnish person has served on the Modern Hebrew New Testament translation committee!

All of the above demonstrates the miraculous guidance of God in the lives of our family members. If my father were still alive, I would tell him that his predictions did not exactly come to pass. My God, in His mysterious ways, has taken care of both parents and children.

Our Homes in Tiberias

Our first dwelling-place in Tiberias was Dr. Heart's completely vandalized summer home, which we gradually refurbished over the course of our stay with wood products from Finland. The house is about three kilometers north of the city. It was a long and difficult trip for the children to go to school because they had to climb a steep hill without a beaten path. We cleared a narrow path for them through the brambles.

Life in this house eventually became too inconvenient. The YMCA in Jerusalem wanted to take advantage of the opportunity and so a variety of vacationers would be sent to us, from various places. The lifestyle of the visitors made us uncomfortable. I was offered a kind of hotel manager's position for which I would even have received a salary but we thought it best to move when our lease was over.

We were able to rent a very small house in the city that had a kitchen and a bedroom. There was no running water or electricity. There was an outside veranda, but without a roof. The bathroom was in a small sheet-metal shack.

Mirja recalls how on one Sabbath day, a large group of Orthodox youth appeared on our veranda. They couldn't accept the fact that a "missionary" had come to their city. I was in Finland at the time, and Maire was not at home. As such, the youths felt they could act in a threatening manner. More and more of them kept arriving.

The children began to be frightened. The door was locked and there were bars on all the windows. Rauha-Lilja was sent to get help.

She slipped out the window and when the youths demanded to know what she was doing, she began to play with a chicken in the yard. Then when they were no longer paying attention to her, she ran off to the police station to tell them of the danger. The police left immediately but by the time they arrived at the house, the group had scattered.

The police then drove into the city park where the fellows were sitting. One of them was holding a heated speech against missionaries. Three of them were identified as troublemakers and arrested. As they were questioned, their comrades yelled at the police, "So you came to help the missionaries!"

To the credit of the competent police force, I must mention that these types of threats were not repeated.

Two years later we were offered a larger house, formerly a "pension" home for tourists. Although our home at the time was conveniently close to the children's school, the rent was high so we decided to take the offer. This new home was much more spacious for which we were thankful. We lived there for about ten years.

In Israel, private individuals own only about five percent of land. Even *kibbutzes* are on government land. The rental agreement on these properties must be renewed every forty-nine years, in the year of the Jubilee.

In 1963 we were able to purchase a private home. It was in poor condition, and the lot was covered in thorn bushes. There was a lone fig tree on one side of the house. But we were given a good price and considering the 1500 square meters of property around the house, we bought it.

As we cleared away the thorn bushes and replaced them with fruit trees, human bones surfaced from the lower layers of the earth. Our lot was an old cemetery! This did not disturb us but rather confirmed the words of the angel I had seen in 1944 who said, "This is an ancient burial ground of the Jews!" This came true to the letter.

The boundary line of our lot coincides with the city limits of Tiberias. We are truly grateful to the Lord for this peaceful place. It has often come to mind that God surely gave us this home in place of the farm we had "lost" to the Finnish government when we left for Israel. The Lord is never indebted to anyone. He compensates for our true sacrifices many times over, as He says in Luke 18:28-30.

A Ring in the Sea

Because the value of Finnish currency was low during the war, Maire and I gave our wedding rings for the benefit of the Bible work. In their place we had only copper substitutes.

One day, while we yet lived on the shore of the Galilee, Maire and I decided to go for a swim. Suddenly Maire noticed a gold ring on the bottom of the lake, which she handed to me.

"Try it on to see if it fits," she said. "It's too big for me."

It fit me perfectly. The ring had only the Hebrew gold stamp inside. So I have been married to the Savior's home-lake for thirty years now!

Contrary to my Plans

When I was a young lad, I would often go fishing and hunting in the Salminen forest. I used to think to myself that when I grew up, I would build a cabin on the shore of the lake and live a quiet life detached from the hustle and bustle of the outside world. There in the woods, on the lakeside, I would have a peaceful existence, far away from the deceitful world and my cruel stepmother. (These experiences are described in my book *Orphan Olavi's Trials*.)

But the Lord has led my life in an entirely different direction. Here in Israel we live in the very center of the action. Even Finnish tourism has increased here to amazing proportions. In Tiberias there can be hundreds of tourists at a time. We always seem to find friends from among them. Every day we have visitors and sometimes even large groups coming to our home. Fifty of them may come at the same time, occasionally even a hundred guests to whom we try to serve refreshments! This part of our work has been especially taxing on my wife. Almost every evening in the springtime, I speak to groups of Finnish tourists at one of the hotels. The Tiberias "station" certainly has a high "turnover" rate in goods and people and these are consistently increasing.

I no longer have time to be a tour guide as I once was. I get up at around 4:00 A.M. each morning. I enjoy the peacefulness of the early hour and the crisp fresh air. At this time, the tourists are not yet up and about and I can read God's Word in peace and quiet.

When the Lord called me to this work, I decided firmly that as long as I am granted life, I want to read the Word of God. It is the Bread of Life, which everyone needs. Because I desire to distribute it so widely, I myself must know as well as I possibly can the contents of this Book that I am offering to others.

I have read through the Scofield English Bible thirty-five times. From my reading I began to notice translation errors in the Finnish version of the Bible which resulted in my writing a booklet called *Translation Errors in the Old Testament* (in Finnish). Ten thousand copies of it have been distributed and a new edition is in the process. I continue to discover more errors to be noted, on a regular basis. If only there was enough time for everything!

A Busy Day

One morning, according to my custom, I got up at 4:00 A.M. I read, prayed, requested a blessing and strength for the day's work and wrote replies to several urgent letters.

I left the house at 7:30 A.M. for an appointment to guide a group of tourists. I was to be with them for the day and to lead a Bible study for another group that same evening at the Hartman hotel. Our tour that day was especially long and I got home at 7:00 P.M. Tired or not tired, I had made a promise so I had a quick drink of water, changed my clothes and sighed to the Lord for the strength that I felt so much in need of.

After I finished my hour's talk I was relieved with the thought of soon being able to go home. But then someone pushed their way to me and said, "I am the youth pastor of the Imatra congregation (in Finland) and our young people would really like to hear what you just said to this group. They were at dinner during this hour so they could not be present. Could you please speak to them as well?"

I turned to the Lord and said, "I have only a weary body and an empty vessel but help me to give these young people from Your rich storehouse."

And the Lord was faithful. I had enough strength to give another Bible study to this group of interested young people. At 10:00 P.M. I fell into bed, grateful for the Lord's mercy that day.

A Funeral and a Wedding

Several kinds of surprises happen even among tourist groups. Some time ago, a sister from Tampere in Finland, Aune Tammisto, suffered a severe heart attack and she was taken to the Poria hospital.

I was at her bedside when she regained consciousness and realized that she was about to die. She begged fervently that her body not be returned to Finland for burial. She wanted to be left in the earth of the Holy Land.

From the Scottish Mission we were able to buy a burial plot but because the Jews do not use caskets in burying their dead, finding a casket was extremely difficult. I called the head doctor at a Nazareth hospital and through him I was able to get the name of a casket-maker. Fortunately, he had one left.

After the struggle with "red tape" was overcome, including the acquisition of a burial permit, the ceremony was held in the presence of the tourist group. One of the members, a pastor, performed the rites. And so the Finnish pilgrim to the Holy Land was buried en route.

A couple of days later, we had a wedding on the lawn of our yard. The young Finnish couple said their vows under our large fig tree. As they were good friends of ours and especially as Christian friends of Israel, it was a joy for all of us to celebrate their union at our home.

The Work Continues Regardless

You may have heard tragic news from Israel according to which Bible distribution is forbidden in this country. On April 1, 1978, a law came into effect that at first glance seemed very threatening indeed. According to this law, trespassing could result in up to five years in prison and a fine of 50,000 pounds. The crime would be trying to convert a person from his religion to another religion by bribery.

Some have written to us, inquiring whether they can send anything here anymore, including clothing! Others, lamenting the news reports, have feared this to be the end of the Syväntö Bible distribution work.

I want to disclaim such misunderstandings. They are completely groundless. We continue this work as before, regardless of this law. It seems to be simply a mind game. I don't believe that this kind of a law will ever be enforced. It has caused much alarm in the USA as well as in many other places where millions of Christians are helping the Jews in numerous ways.

The Israeli minister of justice has stated in this regard: "No charge can be made without special permission."

We have been carrying out this work for over thirty years. I don't believe that the devil will be able to stop it. He has tried many times over the years but he has always failed in his efforts.

Chapter 19

Israel and Her Neighbors

Aggressor or Victim?

In Finland as in other parts of the world, it is argued that Israel is the aggressor who time and again makes attempts to seize land from the Arabs. Someone recently sent me a newspaper article that states that Israel has attacked the Arabs four times and increased its land area ten-fold!

These are downright ridiculous allegations. First of all, the land of Israel is very small, comprised of 20,000 square kilometers. This is just a tiny fraction of the landmass under Arab control: 13,800,000 square kilometers! This is larger than all of Europe. If we include Russia, Israel is only 0.6% of the area which is under Arab control (twenty-two states).

The situation can be compared to that of an exorbitantly wealthy master who has two hundred houses, while next to his property sits a small cottage and the master would say, "I want that cottage as well. Let's chase the farmer out of the cottage!" These are the parameters of the situation between the Arab nations and Israel. There are over 200 million Arabs surrounding Israel. They own the world's richest oil fields and have enormous financial clout. Only in Kuwait, for example, the income from oil is $1 million every hour of the year! These figures are simply astronomical yet paradoxically, there does not seem to be a single dollar for the Arab refugees. They even resort to appealing to the UN and the USA for aid towards the plight of the refugees! In Finland, 500,000 Karelians were resettled almost painlessly.

The Golan Heights

When Turkish rule over Palestine was crushed in 1917, England and France began to take care of Middle East affairs. The boundaries of Palestine were set. In the Sea of Galilee area, the limits were the western shore of the Sea; the Jordan River to the North; in the South along the mountain ridge about one kilometer from the shore, all the way to the Ein Gev kibbutz; and from Ein Gev to the mouth of the Jordan thirty feet from the water's edge. The Sea of Galilee has always belonged and will always belong to Israel.

When the nation of Israel was born in 1948 the boundaries around the Sea did not change. But Syria installed nests of machine-guns along the narrow strip between Ein Gev to the Jordan in the North. Israeli fishermen would often be victims of sniper-fire not to speak of kidnapping or murder, in addition to regularly stolen fishnets.

I've already related the story of the couple I was able to rescue from a likely fatal destiny. On a later occasion, our boat was not so fortunate. One stormy night it broke loose from its anchor and drifted to the Syrian shore. I called the Finnish Embassy for help since the boat was officially Finnish property and Syria is not at war with Finland. I was told to retrieve the boat myself since the other side of the lake was not actually the official Syrian border.

So I sent a note to the United Nations but they were not able to help either. We never retrieved our boat, and didn't try to get a new one since the effort would take too much of our precious time.

Not until the Six-Day War in 1967 when Israel took control of the whole of the Golan Heights did peace come to the shores of the Sea of Galilee.

In Joshua 13:8, 11 and 12, it is told of how God divided the land with the help of Moses, in 1500 BC. Two and a half Israeli tribes were allocated settlement areas in what is now known as the Golan Heights. In these

Bible passages the areas are listed: "Gilead, and the border of Geshurites and Maachathites, and all Mount Hermon, and Bashan to Salcah." The Bashan region is directly across the other side of the Sea.

On the east side of the Jordan River, the Israelis had three autonomous cities and three on the west side. Behind the lake, on the edge of the desert there was an ancient Israeli city of refuge called Golan. These regions God promised to His own people and no power in the world is able to drive them from there. They have, therefore, settled in their own regions.

A new city has been established in the Golan Heights called Katzrin. It is somewhat above the place where the Jordan flows into the Galilee. It is estimated that 30,000 people will move there within the next five to ten years. Many new roads have also been built for the Golan. These are not for the Syrians but rather for the Israelis!

Samaria *et al*

There has also been continuous talk of Samaria. But there are clear prophecies in God's Word about these regions as well. In Ezekiel 16, there is a remarkable prophecy about Sodom.

We recall how Jesus cursed Capernaum: "And thou, Capernaum, which art exalted unto heaven, shalt be brought down to hell: for if the mighty works, which have been done in thee, had been done in Sodom, it would have remained until this day. But I say unto you, That it shall be more tolerable for the land of Sodom in the day of judgment than for thee" (Matt. 11:23, 24). Capernaum has not been promised a restoration period in the Bible. It is still in ruins, as thousands of tourists have witnessed. Only the ruins of the synagogue are to be seen today at the place where Jesus gave His world-shaking message.

But Sodom is promised a restoration, and that promise is now being fulfilled before our very eyes. In Ezekiel 16:53, 55 it is written:

> When I shall bring again their captivity, the captivity of Sodom and her daughters, and the captivity of Samaria and her daughters, then will I bring again the captivity of thy captives in the midst of them: ...When thy sisters, Sodom and her daughters, shall return to their former estate,

and Samaria and her daughters shall return to their former estate, then thou and thy daughters shall return to your former estate.

In Samaria we find the area of land which Jacob purchased in ages past, as written in the Scriptures. Who would argue that that transaction is no longer in effect? And Jacob dug the well that is there to this day. Also, Joseph was brought from Egypt to be buried near Jacob's well. An edifice that is also still standing marks his tomb. These are samples of Jewish customs found in their own territory.

The prophet Obadiah further qualifies Israel's territorial rights:

And they of the south shall possess the mount of Esau; and they of the plain the Philistines: and they shall possess the fields of Ephraim, and the fields of Samaria: and Benjamin shall possess Gilead (v.19).

In verse twenty they are promised the land of the Canaanites (Phoenicia) as far as Zarephath.

Zarephath is in southern Lebanon. Just a short time ago, the Israelis went specifically to these areas, destroying guerilla bases. This time they had to come back. But according to the Bible, their land will extend to this point. In time, even this prophecy will be fulfilled.

An Abundance of Resources

Israel is a poor country, burdened by overwhelming expenditures including the reception of new immigrants, upkeep of the military, guarding the borders. In this regard, Isaiah 60:5 contains a remarkable promise for Israel: "Then thou shalt see, and flow together, and thine heart shall fear, and be enlarged; because the abundance of the sea shall be converted unto thee, the forces of the Gentiles shall come unto thee."

The Dead Sea is located on the bottom of a large, naturally formed depression in the earth, 395 meters below sea level. This same depression in the earth's surface extends to East Africa where it is known as the Rift Valley, and continues to the shores of the Indian Ocean.

Over the course of thousands of years, the Dead Sea has consistently evaporated. This explains the masses of minerals that have accumulated on the shore. It is only recently that modern technology has recognized the value of these minerals and they have begun to be extracted for profit.

For example, there are enormous amounts of potash in the waters of the Dead Sea. It would be possible to collect one million tons of this material each year, for the next two hundred years. If magnesium were extracted at the rate of one million tons a year, the supply would not be exhausted for 20,000 years. If bromine supplies were exploited at the rate of 15,000 tons a year, they wouldn't be used up for the next 60,000 years. These are downright mind-boggling figures!

In regard to the prophecy about Sodom, that it will return to its former state, this has become a reality in our era. Israel has large chemical factories in Sodom, on the shore of the Dead Sea. Several kinds of raw materials are taken from these salty waters. What will be found when they set to work on the bottom layers of the lake?!

Israel is the chief producer of bromine in the world. Bromine is a certain type of medicine for the nerves, which one factory produces for export. Potash has been a fertilizer product, one of the less-expensive ones, but it is produced in large quantities for export as well. A remarkable material has also been discovered in this area, which can be heated to 4,000 degrees. A factory is currently working three shifts a day, producing it for export.

At present, the sea's treasures are "turning" to Israel, as the prophet prophesied thousands of years ago. In the middle of the desert there is an area enclosed by barbed wire where hundreds of scientists are carrying out experiments in laboratories, trying to discover what raw materials are contained in the Dead Sea and what the most practical way would be to separate them, ready for the world market.

The Dead Sea seems to be a true spring of wealth. Similarly, the *Kalevala* folk tales of Finland tell of the Sampo, a Finnish lake said to have produced a container of food, another of items to sell, another of household goods. It is only a matter of time until scientists will be able to separate the raw materials needed for atomic energy from the Dead Sea. Then they will have the kind of Sampo of which the *Kalevala* heroes sang in days past.

In recent times, rich oil fields have also been discovered in Israel which meet about 13% of the country's oil needs. The government is devoting increasingly greater funds in search of crude oil.

Chapter 20

God's Plan for Israel

A Spiritual Re-Birth

God's plans and Israel's own plans are quite different from each other. The activity that is going on now in the land of Israel is directed only towards financial prosperity and the material well being of the country and its people.

God's plan is to spiritually awaken the people from a condition void of life to a new life, as described in the thirty-seventh chapter of Ezekiel. The mind of the Jewish people is set on the improvement of their temporal life but God's mind is geared toward their spiritual rebirth as well as that of all mankind and the destruction of the power of sin on the earth. Although the Jews strive only toward temporal goals, God plans to use them again, as a great blessing for the peoples of the world.

The Bible speaks of this in Zechariah 8:13 and 23:

> ...as ye were a curse among the heathen, O house of Judah, and house of Israel; so will I save you, and ye shall be a blessing: fear not, but let your hands be strong.
> Thus saith the Lord of hosts; In those days it shall come to pass, that ten men shall take hold out of all languages of the nations, even shall

take hold of the skirt of him that is a Jew, saying, We will go with you: for we have heard that God is with you.

In this last verse a remarkable truth is stated. "God with us" is the meaning of the word Immanuel, the Name of our Lord. Isaiah wrote of Him: "Therefore the Lord himself shall give you a sign; Behold, a virgin shall conceive, and bear a son, and shall call his name Immanuel" (7:14).

When the Jews recognize Immanuel and accept Him to whom this prophetic Name belongs, then God will begin to use them as a blessing to all of mankind. It is prophesied in Isaiah 27:6 in these words: "He shall cause them that come of Jacob to take root: Israel shall blossom and bud, and fill the face of the world with fruit." This certainly refers to more than oranges! When the Bible speaks of the tribe of Jacob or even of Jacob alone, it refers to the entire people of Israel as they are, a still spiritually unrevived people. On the other hand, when it speaks of Israel, it refers to the born-again, the remnant that has been refined in God's school and chosen through His mercy. The Apostle Paul speaks about this in Romans 11:5. Only this "remnant" will be able to fill the entire earth with its fruit.

The word Israel is mentioned 3,138 times in the Bible. God must have something very special to accomplish through this nation since it is mentioned so often in His Word.

Eretz Israel

God Himself has given this land its name that is found from the opening pages of the Bible to its final pages. In the Hebrew Bible, He uses the name *Eretz Israel* or "Land of Israel" in Hebrew. This name is also mentioned in the New Testament when the angel encourages Joseph to "Arise, and take the young child and his mother, and go into the land of Israel: for they are dead which sought the young child's life" (Matt. 2:20).

This land also has another name, Palestine. It is an ugly, derogatory name, its root in the word *Philistea*. On the shores of the Mediterranean lived Israel's worst enemies, the Philistines. They had five cities and their area of settlement was called *Philistea*. Since p and f are the same letter in the Hebrew language, *Philistea* is known today as Palestine. In the Old

Testament this name is used only four times. The last time it is mentioned, it is in connection with God's severe judgments.

These judgments are mentioned in Zephaniah 2:4-7:

> For Gaza shall be forsaken, and Ashkelon a desolation: they shall drive out Ashdod at the noonday, and Ekron shall be rooted up. Woe unto the inhabitants of the sea coast, the nation of the Cherethites! The word of the Lord is against you; O Canaan, the land of the Philistines, I will even destroy thee that there shall be no inhabitant. And the sea coast shall be dwellings and cottages for shepherds, and folds for flocks. And the coast shall be for the remnant of the house of Judah; they shall feed thereupon: in the houses of Ashkelon shall they lie down in the evening: For the Lord their God will visit them, and turn away their captivity.

This is the last time the Bible mentions the word Palestine and today this prophecy has been fulfilled to the last letter. Those cities now belong to Israel, as Zephaniah predicted. It is my opinion that the nation of Palestine will never be born. We have clear prophecies in God's Word that all regions that the Jews had in ancient times will once again be for the Jews. If it were otherwise, God would be a liar, and then everything else would crumble. If we cannot trust God's Word, then God's entire plan of salvation is untrustworthy. But He who does not change, Who in every situation has been revealed as completely trustworthy, has Himself said, "Heaven and earth shall pass away but my Word shall not pass away." Thanks be to God!

Some Divine Promises

In the opening pages of the Bible there are clear promises directed at this land:

> The Lord said unto Abram, after that Lot was separated from him, 'Lift up now thine eyes, and look from the place where thou art northward, and southward, and eastward, and westward:
> For all the land which thou seest, to thee will I give it, and to thy seed forever (Genesis 13:14, 15).

This promise is repeated in Amos 9:14,15.

Someone may claim that Abram had another son as well, Ishmael. Perhaps God was also referring to Ishmael in this passage, and to his descendants? This question is answered in Genesis 17:19: "...And God said, Sarah thy wife shall bear thee a son indeed; and thou shalt call his name Isaac: and I will establish my covenant with him for an everlasting covenant, and with his seed after him." This is stated quite clearly, and settles the whole issue once and for all.

In order that the ownership of the land of Canaan/Palestine be absolutely clear, the Bible tells of how God appeared in a dream to Jacob:

> And behold, the Lord stood above it [the ladder] and said, 'I am the Lord, God of Abraham thy father, and the God of Isaac: the land whereon thou liest, to thee will I give it, and to thy seed;
> And thy seed shall be as the dust of the earth, and thou shalt spread abroad to the west, and to the east, and to the north, and to the south: and in thee and in thy seed shall all the families of the earth be blessed (Genesis 28:13, 14).

Thus Palestine was not intended for Ishmael nor even for Jacob's brother Esau and his descendants, but only for those people who descended from Jacob or Israel, therefore the Israelis.

God announced to Abraham the boundaries of the future kingdom of Israel: "In the same day the Lord made a covenant with Abram, saying, Unto thy seed have I given this land, from the river of Egypt unto the great river, the river Euphrates: The Kenites, and the Kenizzites, and the Kadmonites, and the Hittites, and the Perizzites, and the Rephaims, and the Amorites, and the Canaanites, and the Girgashites and the Jebusites" (Genesis 15:18,19). This promise also appears more than once, also in Exodus 23:31, Deuteronomy 11:24, Joshua 1:3,4. Therefore Israel has not come even close to acquiring the lands which have been promised her by God, to say nothing of taking possession of Arab lands!

Palestine was under Turkish control from 1517 to 1917, and Turkey thoroughly destroyed the land. The persons in power enforced ridiculous, destructive laws. For example, live trees were taxed, resulting in a mass cutting down of beautiful trees. This country was in a truly wretched condition by the end of the Turkish regime. Some have speculated that the Arabs could have, in the matter of a few thousand years, been able to cultivate this land but truthfully speaking this is a very unlikely supposition. Reality has proved the situation to be quite the opposite. This is evident not only from travelers' accounts from this period but also from God's Word, "…and your land shall be desolate…" (Leviticus 26:33).

Here once again, we see God's foresight and wisdom. If this land had been well-cultivated and well-settled, there would not have been space for the Jews to come to when the time was ripe for God to have them return to their own land.

During the Turkish occupation, several large marshes in the land caused malaria in epidemic proportions. The Jisreel valley, for example, fifty kilometers long and ten kilometers wide, from Haifa to Beit Shean, was so infested with the disease that thousands died, particularly in the time when there was no known medicine to fight it. The Jews effectively drained this valley which is also referred to as Armageddon in the Bible, where the decisive battle in the history of the world is yet to be fought (Revelation 16:16).

About fifty years ago, a Jew named Joshua Hankin embarked on a life-long mission: to purchase the Jisreel Valley from an Arab tribe. For this purpose, he had to get in touch with every member of that tribe. He needed the signature of each member and to pay him the required amount of money. Each one assured him that he was satisfied with the transaction. This endeavor took ten years before the sale was final. Thus this valley was bought for a high price. It has since been drained, cultivated and today it is the country's largest source of grain, with 60,000 hectares of excellent arable land.

The city of Afula is in the center of the valley. Prophet Elisha's deceptive servant Gehazi placed the goods he received from Naaman on a "small hill," according to the Finnish translation of 2 Kings 5:24. However, the original language calls the hill *ofek*. Afula is now situated on the site of the ancient village of *ofek*.

The Hula Valley

Another breeding place for malaria mosquitoes was the swamp of the Hula Valley. It was still in its virgin state when our family arrived in this country. Everywhere in the area there were people suffering from malaria. Prophet Isaiah prophesied: "The people that walked in darkness have seen a great light: they that dwell in the land of the shadow of death, upon them hath the light shined" (9:2). This chapter speaks of the Messiah, "the great light," who would bring to glory "the way of the sea, beyond Jordan, in Galilee of the nations," -in other words, the land of the heathen.

The swampland of Hula was "the land of the shadow of death" in the past. When the Bible tells of Jesus' healing Peter's mother-in-law at Capernaum, the Hebrew translation calls her illness malaria. When our family settled on the shores of the Sea of Galilee, we took turns with attacks of the sickness. When Maire was hospitalized for this reason, she was there with fifty others being treated for the same reason.

The State of Israel did a tremendous job of draining the swamp. Even some Finnish volunteer groups were there to help dig ditches. Only a small portion of the area was left as a natural habitat for migrating birds to rest their wings. Papyrus still grows there. It cannot be found anywhere else in the world except here and by the Nile River.

When England's General Allenby took possession of this land from the Turks in 1917, it remained under English control until Israel was established in 1948.

The Lion Statue

A famous Jewish leader, Haim Weizmann, a professor of chemistry, had done a great service to the English government during WWI. He invented smokeless gunpowder and gave it to the English. Jews were already fighting in General Allenby's forces. Allenby did not wish to send his men to the Hula Valley since the risk of malaria was so high. He felt that the swamps should be left to the Turks since they would not be of any use to the nation. In his army there was a Jewish captain, Trumpeldorf, who said that the swamps were also Israeli homeland, belonging to the tribe of Dan and that God had promised this to his people in ages past.

Trumpeldorf left to fight for this territory with volunteer troops and he, along with seven of his comrades, fell in those battles. But the land was conquered. In their memory, a stone monument of a lion has been erected in the north of Israel. Young Israelis pay homage to this monument, on their yearly pilgrimages to holy shrines. The northernmost city in the country, Kiryat Shmona, was named the "eighth city," in memory of these heroes. The city has since filled with new immigrants.

After the Hula and its surrounding swamp areas were drained, it became a region for growing cotton and so a cotton factory has been built in Kiryat Shmona. This city often suffers from missiles sent by the PLO. They are fired haphazardly and they explode wherever they happen to land, causing all kinds of damage. A female Finnish acquaintance of ours has worked there for the past ten years as a mid-wife and occasionally she brings us parts of those missiles to show us, which she has collected from her own yard!

When the patience of the Israelis runs out and they begin to investigate the source of these missiles, the international press raises a big fuss, saying Israel has attacked the Arabs again! But is it not true that if the master of the house sees rocks flying and breaking the windows of his house he will go and see from where these stones are being thrown and to discover what kind of a prankster this could be who does not know when to stop his activities? Any country in a similar situation would not hesitate to react to such crimes, and certainly sooner than Israel has done.

The Arab Christians

There are many Christian Arabs in South Lebanon who have suffered unspeakably at the hands of the PLO. Forty to fifty thousand of them have been killed and over a hundred thousand wounded. Israel has assisted these people in every way. Thousands who have been abused are in Israeli hospitals. Our friend in the north tells us that in their maternity hospital, Arab mothers are the majority. Israel has put in a water system worth millions of pounds, given medicine, grain and everything that is needed for their care.

Before the Christmas of 1977, we also sent nine hundred copies of the Bible as gifts to the Lebanese Christians. A believing Canadian army officer carried a burden on his heart to help them. He had a special permit from the Israeli government to go there and take different types of aid to the local people. It was he who came to ask me for Bibles but he had only a small Fiat. I therefore let him use our Volkswagen mini-bus in order to make only one trip instead of two.

He had received permission to transport some Southern Lebanese leaders to Bethlehem for Christmas. A few days before Christmas, he showed up at our place with a group whom he introduced, saying, "Here now are those leaders on their way to Bethlehem."

We served them coffee and chatted with them for a while. They had endured suffering in many ways. As they left, they thanked us saying, "When this wretched border opens up, we welcome you to come and visit us! Thank you for giving us the Bread of Life for Christmas! This is the best Christmas gift we could receive."

Another false accusation against Israel is the argument that Israel has chased the Arabs from this country. This is not even close to the truth! I arrived in this country at the time of its "birth pangs" and I was a witness to the situation as it developed. It was the Arabs, in their rage at the establishment of the nation of Israel, who began to kill the Jewish people.

And it is not Israel who has attacked the Arabs first. The truth is the opposite. The 1973 Yom Kippur War is one of the testimonies to this fact. The Jews were worshipping on their most important day of the year when the Arabs attacked. This was a ruthless, surprise attack.

The largest tank battle in the world was fought near us, on the other side of the Sea of Galilee. When Hitler began his Russian invasion, he had a thousand tanks on a 500-kilometre front. There were 1200 tanks on a 40-kilometre battlefront about twenty kilometers away from us. But God in his mercy helped us also in these situations.

The Arabs had some amphibious tanks with which they had planned to come straight across the lake, but not one of them was able to reach this side of the shore.

An Influx of Immigrants

Jews from all around the world are arriving at a steady pace. At this time, there are already three million Jews in the land. When the Jews returned from Babylonian captivity, there were 50,000 of them. This new immigration is one of the most unparalleled events in history, prophesied by Jeremiah (among others):

> Therefore, behold, the days come, saith the Lord, that it shall no more be said, 'The Lord liveth, that brought up the children of Israel out of the land of Egypt;
> But, the Lord liveth, that brought up the children of Israel from land of the north, and from all the lands whither he had driven them: and I will bring them again into their land that I gave unto their fathers (Jeremiah 16:14, 15).

God's plan for Israel has been brought forth in many passages in the Bible. Prophet Ezekiel speaks of it in this way:

> When I have brought them again from the people, and gathered them out of their enemies' lands, and am sanctified in them in the sight of many nations;
> Then shall they know that I am the Lord their God, which caused them to be led into captivity among the heathen: but I have gathered them unto their own land, and have left none of them any more there (Ezekiel 39:27, 28).

This land, therefore, belongs to this people, the Jews, and God will take care that they will all be gathered here. The Lord says in His Word that He will send forth many fishermen for this purpose to "fish" them out. But if that doesn't help, He will send many hunters. He has used both methods. When God pulls and the devil pushes, one has to move. Otherwise the result will be disastrous.

What a catastrophe it was during the last World War! Herzl tried in every way to urge German Jews to return to their homeland. They were angry with him and said, "We will never leave this country. Germany is our promised land."

The First Zionist Conference was supposed to have taken place in Munich in 1897, but they said, "We aren't going to allow this type of conference in our city!" So it was held in Basel. It was a remarkable coincidence that Munich was precisely the city where Hitler had his headquarters. It was also in Munich that Jewish athletes were killed during the Olympics several years ago. Perhaps the devil himself had set up his headquarters there!

Herzl said near the end of his life, "With my watch in hand, I await the catastrophe that will confront the German Jews since they have not heeded my warnings."

Today, Herzl's body has been brought to an honored place in Jerusalem. The words of Jesus were true even in this instance, when He said, "Woe unto you! For ye build the sepulchers of the prophets, and your fathers killed them" (Luke 11:47).

Help for the Poor

During the first years of the State of Israel, between 1948 and 1951, 1.5 million new immigrants arrived in this country, all of them poor, desolate refugees. It is generally considered that Jews are wealthy, directors of large companies, scientists. These types of people, however, have generally not wanted to return to the land of the Jews. About 800,000 refugees have come from Arab countries such as Morocco, Algeria, Tunisia, Libya, Egypt, Iraq and Yemen, having lost their possessions in their former homelands. In Egypt alone, Jews left behind an inheritance valued at about $250 million!

The second group of initial immigrants came from communist countries. From Romania, 25,000 elderly people were allowed entry every year. By 1987, 370,000 had arrived from Romania. These immigrants were under such strict regulations by their government that they were not allowed to take with them even their own garments that contained any amount of wool or leather. This was an obvious form of robbery. At this time in Israel, even clothing was rationed and each of these Romanian refugees could take with him only twenty kilos of luggage!

My wife Maire has worked long and hard each day of the year, also distributing clothing from Finland to these poor immigrants. Over a twenty-five year period she clothed thousands of them. The families from the East tend to have many children. Kalervo and Meri have joined us in this work. We tend to do this distribution of clothing in the cold rainy season, from November to April, never giving Bibles at the same time in order to avoid accusations of bribery for the purposes of conversion!

Sowing the Seed

Many remain quite indifferent to the Old Testament. Often, the attitude is, "It contains so much plain history and old tales which don't have any significance for the present!" This is the argument of those who do not know God's plan for the salvation of mankind since the Bible is certainly the most valuable book of reference concerning current affairs in today's day and age. We can follow a great number of prophecies being fulfilled as I write this book.

The Bible Society in Israel has a fine marble building in Haifa. When their director retired recently, he gave a report of the results of his work. According to this document, since the establishment of the state, they have sold 127,000 Bibles and New Testaments in the land.

The Bible Society figure includes those copies that we have purchased from them. Since we need Bibles in several languages and we ourselves could not have printed them all, we acquired them already printed. We have distributed 400,000 copies of the Bible with the New Testament. We thank God for every Bible that has been given in this country.

We are grateful to God that throughout these years we have been able to "sow" among these people a tremendous amount of God's Word, which definitely will not return void. The Lord says,

> For as the rain cometh down, and the snow from heaven, and returneth not thither, but watereth the earth, and maketh it bring forth and bud, that it may give seed to the sower, and bread to the eater:
> So shall my word be that goeth forth out of my mouth: it shall not return unto me void, but it shall accomplish that which I please, and it shall prosper in the thing whereunto I sent it (Isaiah 55:10, 11).

Our primary work here has been this sowing of the seed. When the master gives his hired man a sowing machine and says, "Go and plant that field," the hired man's responsibility is to do just that.

A Prophetic Dream

I had a remarkable dream. I was standing on the shore of the Sea of Galilee and my intention was to go across to the other side. To my great surprise, I realized that the entire lake was covered with ice. Such an incident has never happened in real life. The ice was even covered with heavy snow. The Lord said to me, "You must go to the other side!"

I still recall how heavy and difficult that journey was, tramping the ten kilometers through the snow.

At last I managed to get across. Then I had to climb up the high hill that was on the other side. Maire was with me on this trip. When we were just about to reach the top of the hill before us, we noticed that a huge rock blocked the entire road. I began to wonder how this could be since the road up to that point had been so clearly marked.

We were underneath the tongue of this huge rock. In my dream, I said to Maire, "Let's see what will really come of this since the Lord told us to come here, but the road has been cut off, and we can't get through it all."

We began to pray together, *Dear Heavenly Father! You can see this mighty rock that blocks our way. Help us, Lord, so that we may go forward, to where You have intended that we should go!*

Suddenly the whole cliff began to tremble, the rock above us quivered and began to loosen.

If that rock weighing a ton should fall on us, there won't be anything left of us, I thought in horror. It came down and I didn't have but a moment to think it would be only a matter of seconds before our lives would have ended.

But the situation changed at that moment. The rock turned into rich soil and moved carefully past us, and the road opened before us so that we were able to climb to the top of the hill. A miraculous scene opened up before us from that high place. An enormous field of grain spread out before us as far as the eye could see, and in the background the Sea of Galilee was bathed in sunlight.

"Look, Maire!" I said to my wife. "Look at that view! In time it will produce a record harvest…"

Epilogue

We have continued to hold on to these basic principles which the Lord gave us to guide us in this ministry. We never sell anything and we give the Word only to those who request it. In the beginning we focused our work on giving Bibles to the Jews only, for the most part in Hebrew, but also in other languages to the new immigrants. These were always complete Bibles with the New Testament. But we also distribute New Testaments. In England there is a group called the Society for Distributing the Hebrew Scriptures, which prints bilingual New Testaments, of which one of the languages is necessarily Hebrew. These are a great assistance to new immigrants.

When I came here from London in the summer of 1947, I brought with me the first copies of the first printing of Hebrew/English New Testaments. Since then I have been the representative of that society in Israel. They continue to do blessed work among Jewish communities in various parts of the world.

The traditional "missionary" approach is not appropriate for Israel. Saturday, the Sabbath, is the day of rest. Outdoor meetings are not permitted except with a special permit from the police. Christian worship services are on Sunday that is an ordinary workday here. The Jews cannot be reached through preaching. A second great hindrance is that missions try to "fish" for new members in order to increase the numbers in their respective denominations. The Jews well remember how they have been

Epilogue

persecuted in many so-called Christian countries. Even in Luther's homeland, six million of them were murdered. If they come to believe in Jesus as Yeshua, their Saviour and Messiah, they want to establish their own indigenous congregations here. They call themselves Messianic Jews and correctly so. As of 1987, there are about thirty such groups totaling about three thousand members.

What then, is the best method of work for us Gentiles working with Jews? Let us look at what the Bible says about this. Ezekiel 36:24-27 says that the Lord will sprinkle "clean water" upon them and give them "a new heart and a new spirit." What is this "clean water" which is spoken of in this passage? Isaiah 55:11 explains its meaning: "So shall my Word be that goeth forth from my mouth; it shall not return unto me void..." According to Isaiah 55:1 and 2 it is like water to those who thirst: "Ho, every one that thirsteth, come ye to the waters; and he that hath no money; come ye, buy, and eat; yea, come, buy wine and milk without money and without price." And it is according to this principle that we have toiled here these past decades.

Once we received from Sweden an unusual request for Bibles. The queen of Iran and the crown prince, who resided in Cairo, in Sadat's palace, requested from Sweden, Bibles printed in Persian (Parsi), Turkish and Arabic. Sweden didn't have them so that request was passed on to us, here in Israel! I gladly sent them the requested Bibles and in addition, enclosed a letter in which I urged them to read the New Testament especially. I closed by wishing them God's blessing and protection. I received a nice thank you letter, on the royal letterhead, from the queen. Some time later, I received another letter with the same letterhead from Paris. The crown prince, married to Sadat's daughter, thanked me for those Bibles and reported that they were no longer living in Cairo. A short time later, Sadat was assassinated. The same fate might well have awaited them had they remained in Cairo. I have kept those letters.

There are approximately 400,000 Iranian refugees in Europe, and they now hunger for God's Word. Requests from several directions have come to us to send them the Word of God. When Jews came here to Israel from Iran, we needed Bibles for them as well. By 1987 we printed 12,000 complete Bibles and 18,000 New Testaments in the Parsi language. There is a crying need for these in Iran as well. We continue to send them there.

When Idi Amin was expelled from Uganda, an urgent call came from there for the Word of God. Amin had killed many Christians and destroyed Bibles. I called Finland and spoke with the director of a certain publishing firm and explained to him the situation. I requested 100,000 copies of the Gospel of John in English. They were sent to Uganda as airmail packages which was the only sure, quick way to guarantee their delivery. Shortly afterwards, requests began to arrive from many other countries in Africa, including Cameroon, Ghana, Kenya, Tanzania, Togo, Ivory Coast. Each year we have printed for their needs, 10,000 Bibles, 20,000 New Testaments and 100,000 copies of the Gospel of John, all in English. Nigeria, with a population of 75 million people, is opening up for evangelization and we have been receiving requests for Bibles also from this country.

Some special letters have come to our mailbox. One letter, from a newly converted chief of police, in a rather large city, asks for a Bible, "to each of the policemen in (his) city."

We have also sent and continue to send large amounts of God's Word to India. They too have a great need for the Scriptures. Our work has expanded in much the same manner as that recorded in Acts 1:8, throughout the entire world. We have requests for Persian and Arabic Bibles from as far as the USA. In 1987 alone we printed forty tons of God's Word in seven different languages. The Word will not "return void."

We believe that the State of Israel was born of God's will to fulfill the prophecies in the Bible. In Amos 9:14-15 we read:

> And I will bring again the captivity of my people of Israel, and they shall build the waste cities and inhabit them; and they shall plant vineyards, and drink the wine thereof; they shall also make gardens and eat the fruit of them.
> And I will plant them upon their land, and they shall no more be pulled up out of their land which I have given them,' saith the Lord thy God.

The birth of Israel was a miracle. Even Russia and the United States were in agreement in this instance. The Lord has miraculously assisted and protected Israel for almost forty years to date. I came to this land before

Epilogue

Israel gained independence and thus witnessed first-hand her "birth pangs" and battles.

An important matter was left unresolved back then and it is yet to be resolved: What is Israel's capital city? To the ordinary Christian layperson the answer is perfectly clear: Jerusalem. David made it the capital of Israel already a thousand years before Christ. And it has never been the capital of any Arab nation. Only half of Jerusalem was granted to Israel in 1948. But in 1967, the Lord gave the other half as well into Israel's control. Psalm 122:3 mentions Jerusalem, "builded as a city that is compact together." <u>It cannot and must not be divided</u>. One day it will become the capital city of the whole world, when Christ sits upon the throne of David, His forefather, in Jerusalem (Luke 1:30-33). Jerusalem is mentioned in the Bible 780 times. It has been attacked 46 times and destroyed 17 times. There is a remarkable prophecy about it in Zechariah 12:2,3:

> Behold, I will make Jerusalem a cup of trembling unto all the people round about, when they shall be in the siege both against Judah and against Jerusalem.
> And in that day will I make Jerusalem a burdensome stone for all people: all that burden themselves with it shall be cut in pieces, though all the people of the earth be gathered together against it.

Even the so-called Christian nations have not yet acknowledged Jerusalem as Israel's capital city. As a result, the International Christian Embassy of Jerusalem (ICEJ) was born from among the Christian supporters of Israel. The ICEJ strives to provide unbiased information, to lessen the quarrels between Arabs and Jews, and for many years now has arranged the Christian Feast of Tabernacles in Jerusalem, attended by thousands of friends of Israel from around the world. They are doing a blessed work and the Israeli authorities have reacted to their activities favorably.

In Isaiah 2:1-4 there is a prophecy that touches namely upon this type of activity:

> The word that Isaiah the son of Amoz saw concerning Judah and Jerusalem. And it shall come to pass in the last days, that the mountain of the Lord's house shall be established in the top of the mountains, and shall be exalted above the hills; and all nations shall flow unto it.

And many people shall go and say, Come ye, and let us go up to the mountain of the Lord, to the house of the God of Jacob; and he will teach us of his ways, and we will walk in his paths: for out of Zion shall go forth the law, and the word of the Lord from Jerusalem.

And he shall judge among the nations, and shall rebuke many people: and they shall beat their swords into plowshares, and their spears into pruning hooks; nation shall not lift up sword against nation, neither shall they learn war anymore.

We are urged to pray continually for the peace of Jerusalem. In Isaiah 62:6,7 we read, "I have set watchmen upon thy walls, O Jerusalem, which shall never hold their peace day nor night: ye that make mention of the Lord, keep not silence, And give him no rest, till he establish, and till he make Jerusalem a praise in the earth." There will be no peace in the world until the <u>Prince of Peace</u> sits on the throne of David <u>in Jerusalem</u>.

Billy Graham came here once to hold revival meetings. The reporters cornered him in the King David Hotel and asked him difficult questions, including: "What in your opinion is the best solution for the critical Middle East situation?" Billy Graham was silent for a short while. He apparently asked the Lord for the correct reply. Then referring to Matthew 24:37-39 he said:

The biggest problem of all mankind is <u>sin</u> and its consequences. Mankind's <u>greatest need</u> is <u>redemption from sin</u>. Your nation's gift is right here. From this city, through your Messiah, Jesus Christ, came redemption for the entire world. <u>He</u> is the only <u>Prince of Peace</u> who can give peace to the individual and also to the nations. And only when you <u>as a nation</u> accept Him will there come peace into the whole world.

www.ingramcontent.com/pod-product-compliance
Lightning Source LLC
Chambersburg PA
CBHW071445150426
43191CB00008B/1242